Genesis

Part Two

Genesis 25:19–50:26

Joan E. Cook

with Little Rock Scripture Study staff

Little Rock
Scripture Study

A ministry of the Diocese of Little Rock
in partnership with Liturgical Press

Nihil obstat for the commentary text by Joan E. Cook: Reverend Robert C. Harren, *Censor deputatus.*
Imprimatur for the commentary text by Joan E. Cook: ✟ Most Reverend John F. Kinney, Bishop of St. Cloud, Minnesota, December 17, 2010.

Cover design by Ann Blattner. Interior art by Ned Bustard. Maps by Clifford M. Yeary.

 This symbol indicates material that was created by Little Rock Scripture Study to supplement the biblical text and commentary. Some of these inserts first appeared in the *Little Rock Catholic Study Bible*; others were created specifically for this book by Clifford M. Yeary.

1	2	3	4	5	6	7	8	9

Library of Congress Cataloging-in-Publication Data

Names: Cook, Joan E.
Title: Genesis / Joan E. Cook with Little Rock Scripture Study staff.
Other titles: Bible. Genesis. English. New American. 2018.
Description: Collegeville, Minnesota : Liturgical Press, 2018– | Series: Little Rock Scripture Study.
Identifiers: LCCN 2018028646 (print) | LCCN 2018047300 (ebook) | ISBN 9780814663950 (ebook) | ISBN 9780814663707 (pt. one) | ISBN 9780814663714 (pt. two)
Subjects: LCSH: Bible. Genesis—Textbooks. | Bible. Genesis—Study and teaching—Catholic Church. | Catholic Church—Doctrines.
Classification: LCC BS1233 (ebook) | LCC BS1233 .N43 2018 (print) | DDC 222/.11052056—dc23
LC record available at https://lccn.loc.gov/2018028646

Office of the Bishop

DIOCESE OF LITTLE ROCK

2500 North Tyler Street • P.O. Box 7565 • Little Rock, Arkansas 72217 • (501) 664-0340 Fax (501) 664-6304

Dear Friends,

The Bible is a gift of God to the church, the people gathered around the world throughout the ages in the name of Christ. God uses this sacred writing to continue to speak to us in all times and places.

I encourage you to make it your own by dedicated prayer and study with others and on your own. Little Rock Scripture Study is a ministry of the Catholic Diocese of Little Rock. It provides the tools you need to faithfully understand what you are reading, to appreciate its meaning for you and for our world, and to guide you in a way that will deepen your own ability to respond to God's call.

It is my hope that the Word of God will empower you as Christians to live a life worthy of your call as a child of God.

Sincerely in Christ,

✝ Anthony B. Taylor
Bishop of Little Rock

TABLE OF CONTENTS

Wrap-up lectures are available for each lesson at no charge. The link to these free lectures is LittleRockScripture.org/Lectures/GenesisPartTwo.

Welcome

The Bible is at the heart of what it means to be a Christian. It is the Spirit-inspired word of God for us. It reveals to us the God who created, redeemed, and guides us still. It speaks to us personally and as a church. It forms the basis of our public liturgical life and our private prayer lives. It urges us to live worthily and justly, to love tenderly and wholeheartedly, and to be a part of building God's kingdom here on earth.

Though it was written a long time ago, in the context of a very different culture, the Bible is no relic of the past. Catholic biblical scholarship is among the best in the world, and in our time and place, we have unprecedented access to it. By making use of solid scholarship, we can discover much about the ancient culture and religious practices that shaped those who wrote the various books of the Bible. With these insights, and by praying with the words of Scripture, we allow the words and images to shape us as disciples. By sharing our journey of faithful listening to God's word with others, we have the opportunity to be stretched in our understanding and to form communities of love and learning. Ultimately, studying and praying with God's word deepens our relationship with Christ.

Genesis, Part Two
Genesis 25:19–50:26

The resource you hold in your hands is divided into five lessons. Each lesson involves personal prayer and study using this book *and* the experience of group prayer, discussion, and wrap-up lecture.

If you are using this resource in the context of a small group, we suggest that you meet five times, discussing one lesson per meeting. Allow about 90 minutes for the small group gathering. Small groups function best with eight to twelve people to ensure good group dynamics and to allow all to participate as they wish.

WHAT MATERIALS WILL YOU USE?

The materials in this book include:

- The text of Genesis, chapters 25:19–50:26, using the New American Bible, Revised Edition as the translation.

- Commentary by Joan E. Cook (which has also been published separately as part of the New Collegeville Bible Commentary series).

- Occasional inserts  highlighting elements of the chapters of Genesis being studied. Some of these appear also in the *Little Rock Catholic Study Bible* while others are supplied by staff writers.

- Questions for study, reflection, and discussion at the end of each lesson.

- Opening and closing prayers for each lesson, as well as other prayer forms available in the closing pages of the book.

In addition, there are wrap-up lectures available for each lesson. Your group may choose to purchase a DVD containing these lectures or make use of the audio or video lectures online at no charge. The link to these free lectures is: LittleRockScripture.org/Lectures/GenesisPartTwo. Of course, if your group has access to qualified speakers, you may choose to have live presentations.

Each person will need a current translation of the Bible. We recommend the *Little Rock Catholic Study Bible*, which makes use of the New American Bible, Revised Edition. Other translations, such as the New Jerusalem Bible or the New Revised Standard Version: Catholic Edition, would also work well.

HOW WILL YOU USE THESE MATERIALS?

Prepare in advance

Using Lesson One as an example:

- Begin with a simple prayer like the one found on page 11.

- Read the assigned material in the printed book for Lesson One (pages 12–25) so that you are prepared for the weekly small group session. You may do this assignment by reading a portion over a period of several days (effective and manageable) or by preparing all at once (more challenging).

- Answer the questions, Exploring Lesson One, found at the end of the assigned reading, pages 26–27.

- Use the Closing Prayer on page 28 when you complete your study. This prayer may be used again when you meet with the group.

Meet with your small group

- After introductions and greetings, allow time for prayer (about 5 minutes) as you begin the group session. You may use the prayer found on page 11 (also used by individuals in their preparation) or use a prayer of your choosing.

- Spend about 45–50 minutes discussing the responses to the questions that were prepared in advance. You may also develop your discussion further by responding to questions and interests that arise during the discussion and faith-sharing itself.

- Close the discussion and faith-sharing with prayer, about 5–10 minutes. You may use the Closing Prayer at the end of each lesson or one of your choosing at the end of the book. It is important to allow people to pray for personal and community needs and to give thanks for how God is moving in your lives.

- Listen to or view the wrap-up lecture associated with each lesson (15–20 minutes). You may watch the lecture online, use a DVD, or provide a live lecture by a qualified local speaker. This lecture provides a common focus for the group and reinforces insights from each lesson. You may view the lecture together at the end of the session or, if your group runs out of time, you may invite group members to watch the lecture on their own time after the discussion.

Above all, be aware that the Holy Spirit is moving within and among you.

Genesis

Part Two

LESSON ONE

Introduction and Genesis 25:19–30:24

Begin your personal study and group discussion with a simple and sincere prayer such as:

Prayer

God of my ancestors in faith, open my eyes and ears and heart as I reflect on these people whom you called centuries ago.

Read the Introduction on pages 12–13 and the Bible text of Genesis 25:19–30:24 found in the outside columns of pages 14–25, highlighting what stands out to you.

Read the accompanying commentary to add to your understanding.

Respond to the questions on pages 26–27, Exploring Lesson One.

The Closing Prayer on page 28 is for your personal use and may be used at the end of group discussion.

INTRODUCTION

Welcome to the second half of Genesis in the Little Rock Scripture Study series, exploring in depth Genesis 25:19–50:26, using the associated sections of commentary from Joan E. Cook (originally appearing in the New Collegeville Bible Commentary, *Genesis*). The first half of this study covered Genesis 1:1–25:18, using the same commentary.

Genesis is a story about the beginnings of the universe, the human family, and God's people Israel. It focuses our attention on universal themes, especially relationships between God and people and relationships among people. At the same time these themes are expressed in the styles and settings of the ancient Near East, which require some attention as we take up this study. This review will serve as a reminder to those who completed Part One and as a brief introduction to those who are joining the study at this time.

Themes

Genesis introduces several themes that permeate the entire Bible. The first is divine causality, the belief among ancient people that the deities cause everything to happen in life. For the ancient Israelites this means that the one God, revealed as the great "I AM," takes special interest in them. Another theme is the importance of relationships and the appropriate boundaries within these relationships. These boundaries include right relationships between God and people, among peoples, and even extending to the possession of land. The third theme is that of promise and blessing. The Creator promises to remember and care for all of creation, and carries out that promise in spite of the many ways that creatures violate divinely set boundaries.

Ancient Storytelling

Unlike the way we tell stories today, with great attention to the details surrounding the event or person and with an eye toward accuracy, the ancients had different priorities. For them, stories were primarily a way to communicate the *meaning* of an event or person. In nonliterate cultures where people depended almost exclusively on oral communication, stories were told in ways that their listeners would remember and pass down to their descendants. In Genesis, there are even times that an event is recounted more than once, and sometimes in differing ways, in order to emphasize various meanings.

Sources

The book of Genesis in our Bibles is the result of a long process, beginning with many years of oral storytelling in particular locations and situations. The writing process began around the time of King David (approximately 1000 BC) as he tried to unite the twelve tribes into one people, encouraging scribes to write down the stories of their people. As these stories were woven together to form the Pentateuch (the first five books of the Bible, also known as Torah), the flavor of various contributors remained. And as the collection of stories was edited and brought together over several centuries, a unified story emerged that managed to preserve some variances as well.

Scholars in later centuries identify at least four strands of tradition with particular viewpoints and particular names for God. Below is a quick summary to provide a broad understanding of these strands:

- The Yahwist (J) is named for the first letter of this strand's preferred name for God, Yahweh (Jahweh in German). Out of respect for the sacredness of this divine name, many Bible translations substitute the title "Lᴏʀᴅ" in place of "Yahweh." The Yahwist's stories often rely on vivid language to allow readers and listeners to sense God's presence with them.

- The Elohist (E) is named for the first letter of this tradition's preferred name for God, Elohim (associated with a regional term that originally meant "gods"). The stories in this strand developed in the northern part of Israel and tend to focus on the transcendence of God.

- The Deuteronomist (D) strand emerged during and after the Babylonian exile (6th century BC) as God's people grappled with their painful situation. This tradition understood the exile as divine punishment for violation of God's covenant, and its narration of the stories of Israelite ancestors is characterized by formality and cause-and-effect thinking.

- The Priestly (P) strand also attempted to make sense of the experience of exile. This tradition emphasizes the importance of temple worship, the details of rituals, and genealogies of people.

The average reader may not notice these differences and need not be concerned with unraveling the strands of biblical tapestry. However, it is helpful to be aware that God's word is communicated with a variety of styles and emphases throughout Genesis and the rest of the Pentateuch.

Literary Genres

God's people wrote and spoke according to the conventions of their day. In Genesis, we find three main types of ancient writing:

- *Myths* are ancient stories that convey the beliefs and values of the people. The term "myth" does not mean these stories are to be dismissed as "make-believe." Rather, these are powerful religious stories that communicate essential truths of God's creative and sustaining actions in the world.

- *Sagas* are stories that tell about the past and relate it to the present. Sagas in Genesis include the stories of creation as well as the familial stories found throughout the book.

- *Genealogies* emphasize the relationships between generations. Most scholars believe these lists are among the latest parts of the book, added centuries later during the exile to produce a record of who belonged to the group exiled from the Promised Land.

Birth of Esau and Jacob

¹⁹These are the descendants of Isaac, son of Abraham; Abraham begot Isaac. ²⁰Isaac was forty years old when he married Rebekah, the daughter of Bethuel the Aramean of Paddan-aram and the sister of Laban the Aramean. ²¹Isaac entreated the LORD on behalf of his wife, since she was sterile. The LORD heard his entreaty, and his wife Rebekah became pregnant. ²²But the children jostled each other in the womb so much that she exclaimed, "If it is like this, why go on living!" She went to consult the LORD, ²³and the LORD answered her:

Two nations are in your womb,
> two peoples are separating while still
> > within you;
But one will be stronger than the other,
> and the older will serve the younger.

²⁴When the time of her delivery came, there were twins in her womb. ²⁵The first to emerge was reddish, and his whole body was like a hairy mantle; so they named him Esau. ²⁶Next his brother came out, gripping Esau's heel; so he was named Jacob. Isaac was sixty years old when they were born.

²⁷When the boys grew up, Esau became a skillful hunter, a man of the open country; whereas Jacob was a simple man, who stayed among the tents. ²⁸Isaac preferred Esau, because he was fond of game; but Rebekah preferred Jacob. ²⁹Once,

continue

THE ANCESTRAL STORY
PART 2: ISAAC AND REBEKAH

Genesis 25:19–28:9

25:19-28 The births of Esau and Jacob

The stories about Isaac are far fewer than those about Abraham. Many of them are incorporated into the narratives about his father Abraham and his sons Jacob and Esau. The Isaac account continues the theme of divine promise of descendants and land. In the narrative the betrothal and barren mother type scenes reappear, as does the wife-sister motif.

In addition, we meet here another motif that occurs throughout Genesis: that of the younger before the older. We will discuss these as we come to them in the Isaac stories.

After a brief genealogical note we learn that Rebekah, like Sarah before her, is sterile—an immediate threat to the promise, just as in the Abraham and Sarah saga. This time the childlessness is quickly overcome when Isaac prays to God and Rebekah becomes pregnant. Her pregnancy, however, is not without difficulty. She carries twins who jostle each other in the womb, making her pregnancy very uncomfortable. Rebekah brings her concern to the Lord, and the divine response confirms that she will bear twins who will father opposing nations; indeed the tension between them has already begun in Rebekah's womb. The Lord informs Rebekah that the older will serve the younger, an unusual arrangement in ancient Near Eastern families.

The story follows the plot of the barren mother type scene: the childless Rebekah has a son (Jacob) and takes steps to insure his success. This account follows the request model, in which Isaac asks God for a son for his wife, and the Lord grants his request. The story alludes to the competition model as well, in the struggle between the two boys. Rebekah does not have a rival wife, but she carries the strife between her two sons even before they are born. The divine response to her prayer in the face of her difficult pregnancy explains the conflict, confirms that it is of divine origin, and announces the reversal of roles between the two brothers. This divine word forms the backdrop for all Rebekah's actions to ensure the success of her younger son Jacob.

In addition, the story alludes to the promise model in the divine explanation to Rebekah while her sons are still in her womb. The threefold promise announces that the tension between the two boys will continue throughout their lives: they will form two different nations; they will struggle for power; and their roles in the family will be reversed.

When the twins are born, Esau comes first, followed by his brother Jacob. Their names foreshadow the defining characteristics of each: Esau is hairy and reddish, and Jacob is the heel-gripper. With their contrasting personalities the two appeal to different parents: Esau the impetuous outdoorsman is his father's favorite while his mother prefers Jacob, the methodical and conniving tent-dweller.

25:29-34 Esau sells his birthright

The first illustration of the boys' contrasting personalities comes when Jacob is preparing a stew. Esau refers to it as "red stuff"; the narrative calls it lentil stew (v. 34). We recall that when Esau was born he was reddish, probably a reference to a ruddy complexion (v. 25). Here the color of the stew attracts his attention; perhaps he thinks it contains blood, which would appeal to his hunter's tastes. In fact, the color comes from the lentils, which would appeal to a vegetarian.

Jacob seizes the opportunity to strike a bargain with his brother, and agrees to give him a bowl of stew in exchange for Esau's birthright. This is a hard bargain, considering the inequality of the tradeoff. It highlights both Jacob's scheming personality and Esau's utter lack of concern for a matter with long-term implications. It also foreshadows Jacob's deception of his father Isaac when he arranges to receive the blessing intended for his brother Esau in chapter 27.

when Jacob was cooking a stew, Esau came in from the open country, famished. [30]He said to Jacob, "Let me gulp down some of that red stuff; I am famished." That is why he was called Edom. [31]But Jacob replied, "First sell me your right as firstborn." [32]"Look," said Esau, "I am on the point of dying. What good is the right as firstborn to me?" [33]But Jacob said, "Swear to me first!" So he sold Jacob his right as firstborn under oath. [34]Jacob then gave him some bread and the lentil stew; and Esau ate, drank, got up, and went his way. So Esau treated his right as firstborn with disdain.

CHAPTER 26

Isaac and Abimelech

[1]There was a famine in the land, distinct from the earlier one that had occurred in the days of Abraham, and Isaac went down to Abimelech, king of the Philistines in Gerar. [2]The LORD appeared to him and said: Do not go down to Egypt, but camp in this land wherever I tell you. [3]Sojourn in this land, and I will be with you and bless you; for to you and your descendants I will give all these lands, in fulfillment of the oath that I swore to your father Abraham. [4]I will make your descendants as numerous as the stars in the sky, and I will give them all these lands, and in your descendants all the nations of the earth will find blessing— [5]this because Abraham obeyed me,

continue

26:1-35 Rebekah endangered

The narrative returns to Isaac, who must care for his family in the midst of a famine. Just as his father did previously, Isaac prepares to migrate in search of food. Egypt is not an option for him because the Lord insists that he stay in the land of promise. At this point the Lord repeats to Isaac the promise of descendants, a nation, and land that was made so many times to Abraham. Instead of going to Egypt, Isaac travels to Gerar, as Abraham did during the second famine (ch. 20).

keeping my mandate, my commandments, my ordinances, and my instructions.

⁶So Isaac settled in Gerar. ⁷When the men of the place asked questions about his wife, he answered, "She is my sister." He was afraid that, if he called her his wife, the men of the place would kill him on account of Rebekah, since she was beautiful. ⁸But when they had been there for a long time, Abimelech, king of the Philistines, looked out of a window and saw Isaac fondling his wife Rebekah. ⁹He called for Isaac and said: "She must certainly be your wife! How could you have said, 'She is my sister'?" Isaac replied, "I thought I might lose my life on her account." ¹⁰"How could you have done this to us!" exclaimed Abimelech. "It would have taken very little for one of the people to lie with your wife, and so you would have brought guilt upon us!" ¹¹Abimelech then commanded all the people: "Anyone who maltreats this man or his wife shall be put to death."

¹²Isaac sowed a crop in that region and reaped a hundredfold the same year. Since the LORD blessed him, ¹³he became richer and richer all the time, until he was very wealthy. ¹⁴He acquired flocks and herds, and a great work force, and so the Philistines became envious of him. ¹⁵The Philistines had stopped up and filled with dirt all the wells that his father's servants had dug back in the days of his father Abraham. ¹⁶So Abimelech said to Isaac, "Go away from us; you have become far too numerous for us." ¹⁷Isaac left there and camped in the Wadi Gerar where he stayed. ¹⁸Isaac reopened the wells which his father's servants had dug back in the days of his father Abraham and which the Philistines had stopped up after Abraham's death; he gave them names like those that his father had given them. ¹⁹But when Isaac's servants dug in the wadi and reached spring water in their well, ²⁰the shepherds of Gerar argued with Isaac's shepherds, saying, "The water belongs to us!" So he named the well Esek, because they had quarreled there. ²¹Then they dug another well, and they argued over that one too; so he named it Sitnah. ²²So he moved on from there and dug still another well,

continue

In verse 6 the wife-sister motif appears again, in the same location, Gerar, that was problematic for Abraham and Sarah in chapter 20. This time there is no prior arrangement between Isaac and Rebekah; the narrative simply tells us that Isaac identifies Rebekah as his sister when the men of Gerar approach him because of her. (Like Sarah, Rebekah is beautiful.) Isaac's first concern is for his own safety, as was Abraham's before him; he fears for his life at the hands of the inhabitants of Gerar.

This time there is no attempt on the part of Abimelech the king to take Rebekah; instead, he happens to see Isaac and Rebekah enjoying each other as husband and wife. The Hebrew word that describes their action comes from the same root as the word "Isaac," which means "laughter" and recalls the joy of Isaac's parents at his birth. But the moment creates the opposite of joy for Abimelech when he realizes that Rebekah and Isaac are husband and wife. The conversation that follows between Abimelech and Isaac shows that Isaac's fears are in vain. Abimelech has no intention of violating Isaac's wife, and he forbids his people to mistreat either of them. This mandate confirms Isaac's earlier fear: the people might indeed have violated Rebekah. It also highlights Isaac's duplicity: if the people had violated Rebekah, it would have been Isaac's fault.

The next episode describes a second incident when tensions arise between Isaac and Abimelech. This time the cause is Isaac's hugely successful farming in Gerar. In an effort to drive him away the Philistines stop up the wells that Abraham dug, and Abimelech directly asks him to leave. Isaac moves to the area where Abraham stayed (21:34), re-digs his father's wells, and discovers a spring in one of them. This valuable water source causes a new round of conflict, so Isaac moves again and digs other wells. These incidents highlight the scarcity of water in the region, and the desire of each family to protect its water sources, particularly during a famine.

Eventually (v. 23) Isaac returns to Beersheba, where he had lived with his father Abraham. Here the Lord appears to him and repeats the promise of descendants. Isaac builds an altar to mark the place where the Lord appeared, just as his father had done. After praying to the Lord, he sets about digging a well. Again he must reckon with Abimelech, who recognizes the power that Isaac has accrued by his economic success. In verse 26 Abimelech and his men ask for a nonaggression pact between the two peoples. Isaac agrees, and they make a formal agreement. A brief genealogical note follows in verse 34, listing Esau's marriages to a Hittite woman and a Hivite woman, a cause of bitterness to his parents. It foreshadows Rebekah's determination that Jacob, not Esau, will receive Isaac's blessing now that Esau has married outside the family.

27:1–28:9 Isaac blesses Jacob

The saga continues as Isaac arranges to bestow his blessing on his son before he dies, like Abraham before him. This episode, in which Rebekah helps Jacob to usurp the blessing intended for Esau, takes place in seven steps, permeated by the motif of younger-older.

The first step (vv. 1-4) involves Isaac and Esau. We learn that Isaac's eyesight is failing, and he instructs his son Esau to hunt game with which to prepare him a meal, so Esau might receive his father's blessing. The formality of the request is evident in several details: first, Esau responds with "Here I am!" the formal acknowledgment of readiness and willingness. In addition, the meal his father requests has a ritual connotation; here it suggests a formal ceremony for bestowing the blessing.

The second step (vv. 5-17) involves the other two people, Rebekah and Jacob. Rebekah repeats what she heard Isaac say to Esau, adding the solemn words, "with the LORD's approval." She quickly formulates a plan and explains it to Jacob. She brushes aside his hesitation because she remembers the Lord's words, "the older will serve the younger," when the twins were still in her womb (25:23). They both make the necessary preparations, and Rebekah sends him in to his father.

The third step (vv. 18-29) takes place between Isaac and Jacob. Jacob lies to his father

but over this one they did not argue. He named it Rehoboth, and said, "Because the LORD has now given us ample room, we shall flourish in the land."

²³From there Isaac went up to Beer-sheba. ²⁴The same night the LORD appeared to him and said: I am the God of Abraham, your father. Do not fear, for I am with you. I will bless you and multiply your descendants for the sake of Abraham, my servant. ²⁵So Isaac built an altar there and invoked the LORD by name. After he had pitched his tent there, Isaac's servants began to dig a well nearby.

²⁶Then Abimelech came to him from Gerar, with Ahuzzath, his councilor, and Phicol, the general of his army. ²⁷Isaac asked them, "Why have you come to me, since you hate me and have driven me away from you?" ²⁸They answered: "We clearly see that the LORD has been with you, so we thought: let there be a sworn agreement between our two sides—between you and us. Let us make a covenant with you: ²⁹you shall do no harm to us, just as we have not maltreated you, but have always acted kindly toward you and have let you depart in peace. So now, may you be blessed by the LORD!" ³⁰Isaac then made a feast for them, and they ate and drank. ³¹Early the next morning they exchanged oaths. Then Isaac sent them on their way, and they departed from him in peace.

³²That same day Isaac's servants came and informed him about the well they had been digging; they told him, "We have reached water!" ³³He called it Shibah; hence the name of the city is Beer-sheba to this day. ³⁴When Esau was forty years old, he married Judith, daughter of Beeri the Hittite, and Basemath, daughter of Elon the Hivite. ³⁵But they became a source of bitterness to Isaac and Rebekah.

CHAPTER 27

Jacob's Deception

¹When Isaac was so old that his eyesight had failed him, he called his older son Esau and said to him, "My son!" "Here I am!" he replied. ²Isaac then said, "Now I have grown old. I do not know

continue

when I might die. ³So now take your hunting gear—your quiver and bow—and go out into the open country to hunt some game for me. ⁴Then prepare for me a dish in the way I like, and bring it to me to eat, so that I may bless you before I die."

⁵Rebekah had been listening while Isaac was speaking to his son Esau. So when Esau went out into the open country to hunt some game for his father, ⁶Rebekah said to her son Jacob, "Listen! I heard your father tell your brother Esau, ⁷'Bring me some game and prepare a dish for me to eat, that I may bless you with the Lord's approval before I die.' ⁸Now, my son, obey me in what I am about to order you. ⁹Go to the flock and get me two choice young goats so that with these I might prepare a dish for your father in the way he likes. ¹⁰Then bring it to your father to eat, that he may bless you before he dies." ¹¹But Jacob said to his mother Rebekah, "But my brother Esau is a hairy man and I am smooth-skinned! ¹²Suppose my father feels me? He will think I am making fun of him, and I will bring on myself a curse instead of a blessing." ¹³His mother, however, replied: "Let any curse against you, my son, fall on me! Just obey me. Go and get me the young goats."

¹⁴So Jacob went and got them and brought them to his mother, and she prepared a dish in the way his father liked. ¹⁵Rebekah then took the best clothes of her older son Esau that she had in the house, and gave them to her younger son Jacob to wear; ¹⁶and with the goatskins she covered up his hands and the hairless part of his neck. ¹⁷Then she gave her son Jacob the dish and the bread she had prepared.

¹⁸Going to his father, Jacob said, "Father!" "Yes?" replied Isaac. "Which of my sons are you?" ¹⁹Jacob answered his father: "I am Esau, your firstborn. I did as you told me. Please sit up and eat some of my game, so that you may bless me." ²⁰But Isaac said to his son, "How did you get it so quickly, my son?" He answered, "The Lord, your God, directed me." ²¹Isaac then said to Jacob, "Come closer, my son, that I may feel you, to learn whether you really are my son Esau or not." ²²So Jacob moved up closer to his father. When Isaac felt him, he said, "Although the voice is Jacob's, the hands are Esau's." ²³(He failed to identify him because his hands were hairy, like those of his brother Esau; so he blessed him.) ²⁴Again Isaac said, "Are you really my son Esau?" And Jacob said, "I am." ²⁵Then Isaac said, "Serve me, my son, and let me eat of the game so that I may bless you." Jacob served it to him, and Isaac ate; he brought him wine, and he drank. ²⁶Finally his father Isaac said to him, "Come closer, my son, and kiss me." ²⁷As Jacob went up to kiss him, Isaac smelled the fragrance of his clothes. With that, he blessed him, saying,

"Ah, the fragrance of my son
   is like the fragrance of a field
      that the Lord has blessed!
²⁸May God give to you
   of the dew of the heavens
And of the fertility of the earth
   abundance of grain and wine.
²⁹ May peoples serve you,
   and nations bow down to you;
Be master of your brothers,
   and may your mother's sons bow down to
      you.
Cursed be those who curse you,
   and blessed be those who bless you."

³⁰Jacob had scarcely left his father after Isaac had finished blessing him, when his brother Esau came back from his hunt. ³¹Then he too prepared a dish, and bringing it to his father, he said, "Let my father sit up and eat some of his son's game, that you may then give me your blessing." ³²His father Isaac asked him, "Who are you?" He said, "I am your son, your firstborn son, Esau." ³³Isaac trembled greatly. "Who was it, then," he asked, "that hunted game and brought it to me? I ate it all just before you came, and I blessed him. Now he is blessed!" ³⁴As he heard his father's words, Esau burst into loud, bitter sobbing and said, "Father, bless me too!" ³⁵When Isaac said, "Your

continue

in order to receive the blessing intended for his brother. Because Isaac is losing his eyesight, he does not recognize Jacob, but questions the voice that sounds like Esau's. He blesses Jacob, assuring him of prosperity, political and military power, and divine protection.

The fourth step (vv. 30-41) brings together Isaac and Esau for the second time, when Esau returns after making the preparations his father directed. He and Isaac both realize what has happened, but it is too late to retract the blessing that has been given to Jacob. When Esau pleads for a blessing for himself, Isaac responds with the blessing of prosperity. He then announces that Esau will live a life of violence and subservience to his brother until he breaks free of him. Esau makes up his mind to kill his brother once their father is dead.

The fifth step (vv. 42-45) brings together Jacob and Rebekah for the second time. She urges him to leave at once and go to her brother Laban rather than risk being killed by Esau. She fears losing both of her sons at once: Jacob if Esau kills him, and Esau if he is condemned for killing his brother.

The sixth step (v. 46) takes place between Rebekah and Isaac. Rather than admit to her husband that she masterminded the deceitful events, she picks up the theme of 26:34-35: Esau's marriages outside the family have brought grief to his parents. Rebekah wants assurance that Jacob will marry within the family, to avoid further sorrow. Her request to send Jacob away has the added advantage of protecting the promise of children and land.

The seventh step (28:1-5) brings together Isaac and Jacob for the second time. Isaac formally sends Jacob to Rebekah's brother Laban to find a wife for himself. He repeats to Jacob the divine promise of land, children, and a nation in the name of his father Abraham, and Jacob sets out on the journey. This is the first time Jacob receives the promise; it comes from his father Isaac.

The episode brings out the deceptive aspect of Jacob's character even more strongly than the incident with the stew. Here Jacob deliberately lies to his father (at the encouragement

brother came here by a ruse and carried off your blessing," [36]Esau exclaimed, "He is well named Jacob, is he not! He has supplanted me twice! First he took away my right as firstborn, and now he has taken away my blessing." Then he said, "Have you not saved a blessing for me?" [37]Isaac replied to Esau: "I have already appointed him your master, and I have assigned to him all his kindred as his servants; besides, I have sustained him with grain and wine. What then can I do for you, my son?" [38]But Esau said to his father, "Have you only one blessing, father? Bless me too, father!" and Esau wept aloud. [39]His father Isaac said in response:

"See, far from the fertile earth
   will be your dwelling;
      far from the dew of the heavens above!
[40]By your sword you will live,
   and your brother you will serve;
But when you become restless,
   you will throw off his yoke from your
      neck."

[41]Esau bore a grudge against Jacob because of the blessing his father had given him. Esau said to himself, "Let the time of mourning for my father come, so that I may kill my brother Jacob." [42]When Rebekah got news of what her older son Esau had in mind, she summoned her younger son Jacob and said to him: "Listen! Your brother Esau intends to get his revenge by killing you. [43]So now, my son, obey me: flee at once to my brother Laban in Haran, [44]and stay with him a while until your brother's fury subsides— [45]until your brother's anger against you subsides and he forgets what you did to him. Then I will send for you and bring you back. Why should I lose both of you in a single day?"

Jacob Sent to Laban

[46]Rebekah said to Isaac: "I am disgusted with life because of the Hittite women. If Jacob also should marry a Hittite woman, a native of the land, like these women, why should I live?"

continue

CHAPTER 28

¹Isaac therefore summoned Jacob and blessed him, charging him: "You shall not marry a Canaanite woman! ²Go now to Paddan-aram, to the home of your mother's father Bethuel, and there choose a wife for yourself from among the daughters of Laban, your mother's brother. ³May God Almighty bless you and make you fertile, multiply you that you may become an assembly of peoples. ⁴May God extend to you and your descendants the blessing of Abraham, so that you may gain possession of the land where you are residing, which he assigned to Abraham." ⁵Then Isaac sent Jacob on his way; he went to Paddan-aram, to Laban, son of Bethuel the Aramean, and brother of Rebekah, the mother of Jacob and Esau.

⁶Esau noted that Isaac had blessed Jacob when he sent him to Paddan-aram to get himself a wife there, and that, as he gave him his blessing, he charged him, "You shall not marry a Canaanite woman," ⁷and that Jacob had obeyed his father and mother and gone to Paddan-aram. ⁸Esau realized how displeasing the Canaanite women were to his father Isaac, ⁹so Esau went to Ishmael, and in addition to the wives he had, married Mahalath, the daughter of Abraham's son Ishmael and sister of Nebaioth.

Jacob's Dream at Bethel

¹⁰Jacob departed from Beer-sheba and proceeded toward Haran. ¹¹When he came upon a certain place, he stopped there for the night, since the sun had already set. Taking one of the stones at the place, he put it under his head and lay down in that place. ¹²Then he had a dream: a stairway rested on the ground, with its top reaching to the heavens; and God's angels were going up and down on it. ¹³And there was the LORD standing beside him and saying: I am the LORD, the God of Abraham your father and the God of Isaac; the land on which you are lying I will give to you and your descendants. ¹⁴Your descendants will be like the dust of the earth, and through them you will

continue

of his mother) in order to get what he wants. It is true that the Lord intends for Jacob to win out over his brother. The means to this end are questionable, though, and Jacob's deception will come back to haunt him. The incident also highlights the extent of Esau's bitterness at his own situation. He arranges to marry one of Ishmael's daughters, to exacerbate his parents' displeasure with him. In addition, in this scene Isaac passes on the promise of descendants, land, and nation to his son Jacob. The event marks the successful completion of Isaac's primary role: he has carried the promise forward to the next generation and entrusted it to the son chosen by God.

Here the narrative leaves Isaac and focuses on Jacob until it announces Isaac's death in 35:27-29. We learn of Jacob's journey to his uncle Laban, his marriages and the births of his children, the tensions between him and Laban, and his meeting with his brother Esau before he returns home. Twice on his journey, once on the way to Haran and once on the way back home, he encounters God.

In the ancient world every achievement and every failure were seen as a direct result of some form of divine intervention. In the Old Testament the **words of blessing** became a tool that called forth divine intervention in the life of an individual or in the larger world. Those who uttered the words were calling down God's active involvement. The words themselves took on a life of their own, actually affecting the person being blessed; their power was not magic but was the result of God's life in them. Because of this divine power, a blessing could not be reversed or taken away. The same was true for **words that cursed**. The deathbed scene with Jacob and his sons illustrates that blessings are often associated with passing on the headship of the family, usually reserved for the firstborn. Throughout Scripture, blessings are also associated with acts of creation

(Gen 1:22, 28), times of crisis (1 Sam 2:20-21; Ruth 4:11-12), protection on a journey (Gen 24:7; Tob 5:17), periods of national transition (Lev 26:3-13), and proclamations of the kingdom of God (Matt 5:3-12; Luke 6:20-26).

THE ANCESTRAL STORY
PART 3: JACOB AND HIS WIVES

Genesis 28:10–36:43

28:10-22 Jacob at Bethel

Just as in the report of the servant's journey to find a wife for Isaac, here we learn only the essentials of Jacob's trip, except for one event that takes place along the way. He stops for the night, apparently out in the open, at a place that has something special about it. There he has a dream in which the Lord gives Jacob the promise of descendants and land. Jacob received that promise from his father before setting out on his journey. Now he receives it directly from God. The deity's name is "Lord," the God of his father and grandfather. This identification makes it clear that, even though Jacob is probably sleeping at a shrine to a local deity, the God who speaks to him there is not the local god but the God who has cared for his family for several generations.

The Lord reiterates the promises of land, descendants, a nation, and divine blessing. When Jacob realizes that he has met the Lord he takes the stone pillow, sets it up vertically, and pours oil on it to designate it as holy because his head rested on it during his revelatory dream. It is thus a witness to the event (see Josh 24:27). Jacob does not build an altar, as his grandfather Abraham did to mark the places where he met the Lord. Instead, he consecrates the stone, then formally accepts the terms of his encounter with God. He names the place Bethel, or House of God, the place near where Abraham once built an altar (12:8).

This story has an element of the E strand in which dreams are an important means of divine communication with humans. Dreaming

spread to the west and the east, to the north and the south. In you and your descendants all the families of the earth will find blessing. [15]I am with you and will protect you wherever you go, and bring you back to this land. I will never leave you until I have done what I promised you.

[16]When Jacob awoke from his sleep, he said, "Truly, the LORD is in this place and I did not know it!" [17]He was afraid and said: "How awesome this place is! This is nothing else but the house of God, the gateway to heaven!" [18]Early the next morning Jacob took the stone that he had put under his head, set it up as a sacred pillar, and poured oil on top of it. [19]He named that place Bethel, whereas the former name of the town had been Luz.

[20]Jacob then made this vow: "If God will be with me and protect me on this journey I am making and give me food to eat and clothes to wear, [21]and I come back safely to my father's house, the LORD will be my God. [22]This stone that I have set up as a sacred pillar will be the house of God. Of everything you give me, I will return a tenth part to you without fail."

CHAPTER 29

Arrival in Haran

[1]After Jacob resumed his journey, he came to the land of the Kedemites. [2]Looking about, he saw a well in the open country, with three flocks of sheep huddled near it, for flocks were watered

continue

is an act beyond human control, which takes place in a realm we cannot access by our own efforts. We often gain valuable insights while dreaming; ancient people understood these as revelations from God.

29:1–30:24 Jacob's marriages

The narrative resumes with Jacob's arrival in the general area of his uncle's home. The plot follows the elements of the betrothal type scene. By looking at those elements we can see from that well. A large stone covered the mouth of the well. ³When all the shepherds were assembled there they would roll the stone away from the mouth of the well and water the sheep. Then they would put the stone back again in its place over the mouth of the well.

⁴Jacob said to them, "My brothers, where are you from?" "We are from Haran," they replied. ⁵Then he asked them, "Do you know Laban, son of Nahor?" "We do," they answered. ⁶He inquired further, "Is he well?" "He is," they answered; "and here comes his daughter Rachel with the sheep." ⁷Then he said: "There is still much daylight left; it is hardly the time to bring the animals home. Water the sheep, and then continue pasturing them." ⁸They replied, "We cannot until all the shepherds are here to roll the stone away from the mouth of the well; then can we water the flocks."

⁹While he was still talking with them, Rachel arrived with her father's sheep, for she was the one who tended them. ¹⁰As soon as Jacob saw Rachel, the daughter of his mother's brother Laban, and the sheep of Laban, he went up, rolled the stone away from the mouth of the well, and watered Laban's sheep. ¹¹Then Jacob kissed Rachel and wept aloud. ¹²Jacob told Rachel that he was her father's relative, Rebekah's son. So she ran to tell her father. ¹³When Laban heard the news about Jacob, his sister's son, he ran to meet him. After embracing and kissing him, he brought him to his house. Jacob then repeated to Laban all these things, ¹⁴and Laban said to him, "You are indeed my bone and my flesh."

Marriage to Leah and Rachel

After Jacob had stayed with him a full month, ¹⁵Laban said to him: "Should you serve me for nothing just because you are a relative of mine? Tell me what your wages should be." ¹⁶Now Laban had two daughters; the older was called Leah, the younger Rachel. ¹⁷Leah had dull eyes, but Rachel was shapely and beautiful. ¹⁸Because Jacob loved Rachel, he answered, "I will serve you seven years for your younger daughter Rachel." ¹⁹Laban replied, "It is better to give her to you than to an-

continue

the story unfold, and can also compare and contrast Jacob's experience with that of Abraham's servant when he went to Haran in search of a wife for Isaac. Jacob arrives at a well that is covered with a large stone, surrounded by several flocks of sheep. Shepherds are with them; when Jacob asks if they know Laban he learns that Laban's daughter Rachel is arriving at that moment with her father's flock.

These details set the stage for a very different experience from that of Abraham's servant who came with a large retinue of gifts for Laban and his family. Jacob comes on the one hand as one sent by God and on the other as a fugitive. He brings nothing with him. Instead, Jacob offers his services, the first of which is to remove the stone from the well. He manages the stone singlehandedly, even though it is huge, because he is thrilled at the sight of Rachel. It is not clear whether he is responding to the sight of a relative or to an attractive young woman; perhaps to both. Then Jacob, instead of asking for water and receiving it from the woman, offers to water Laban's sheep. He further expresses his delight by tearfully kissing Rachel, a gesture of delight and gratitude at meeting his relative (v. 11).

True to the type scene, Rachel hurries to tell her father of Jacob's arrival. He greets the visitor and invites him into his home. Then the narrative tells us only that Jacob told the story of his adventures; it does not repeat Jacob's words as Abraham's servant did.

The arrangements for the betrothal proceed much more slowly here than with Abraham's servant. A month passes before the subject comes up, and then Jacob mentions it in response to Laban's offer to pay Jacob for his services. Jacob offers to work for Laban for seven years in exchange for Rachel's hand (29:18). (Jacob must work for the privilege of marrying Laban's daughter because he does not bring gifts with him, as did Abraham's servant.) The narrative points out that Rachel is the younger of Laban's two daughters, bringing into play the younger-older motif. Jacob meets his match when Laban gives him his older daughter Leah in marriage instead of

Rachel, then falls back on ancient tradition as his excuse for the deceitful arrangement. He assures Jacob that, after the customary seven days of celebration of the first marriage, Jacob may work seven more years for Rachel, and Jacob agrees.

Then the story picks up the barren mother type scene, and the competition model begins to unfold. Two women are married to the same husband; one has children and the other does not. The narrative highlights the divine action on behalf of Leah for her unfavored status. Leah bears four sons: Reuben, Simeon, Levi, and Judah. The names she gives the boys reflect her situation as the unloved wife. The note that she then stops bearing sons foreshadows further difficulties to come.

The request model of the barren mother type scene overlaps with the competition model when Rachel pleads desperately with Jacob to give her children in 30:1. But Jacob does not accept responsibility for her childlessness, and reminds her that children are gifts from God. In her despair she offers her maid Bilhah to Jacob, just as Sarah offered Hagar to Abraham. Rachel arranges that Bilhah will bear surrogate children for her; she clarifies her own maternal status by arranging to hold Bilhah's children on her own knees. The act of holding a child on one's knees legitimates him as the son of that parent (see 48:12 and 50:23). Bilhah bears two sons, whom Rachel names Dan and Naphtali, referring to the competition between her and Leah.

Not to be outdone, Leah then gives her maid Zilpah to Jacob (v. 9). Zilpah bears two sons, giving them names that suggest Leah's own good fortune: Gad and Asher. Jacob now has eight sons, but none by his favored wife Rachel. Leah's son Reuben offers his mother some mandrakes, known for their aphrodisiac qualities. When Rachel asks for some of them she learns of Leah's bitterness at her own unloved status, so Rachel makes a deal: Rachel will have the mandrakes, but Leah will spend the night with Jacob. Leah bears two more sons, whom she names Issachar and Zebulun, reflecting her awkward relationship with Jacob. The narrative

other man. Stay with me." [20]So Jacob served seven years for Rachel, yet they seemed to him like a few days because of his love for her.

[21]Then Jacob said to Laban, "Give me my wife, that I may consummate my marriage with her, for my term is now completed." [22]So Laban invited all the local inhabitants and gave a banquet. [23]At nightfall he took his daughter Leah and brought her to Jacob, and he consummated the marriage with her. [24]Laban assigned his maidservant Zilpah to his daughter Leah as her maidservant. [25]In the morning, there was Leah! So Jacob said to Laban: "How could you do this to me! Was it not for Rachel that I served you? Why did you deceive me?" [26]Laban replied, "It is not the custom in our country to give the younger daughter before the firstborn. [27]Finish the bridal week for this one, and then the other will also be given to you in return for another seven years of service with me."

[28]Jacob did so. He finished the bridal week for the one, and then Laban gave him his daughter Rachel as a wife. [29]Laban assigned his maidservant Bilhah to his daughter Rachel as her maidservant. [30]Jacob then consummated his marriage with Rachel also, and he loved her more than Leah. Thus he served Laban another seven years.

Jacob's Children

[31]When the LORD saw that Leah was unloved, he made her fruitful, while Rachel was barren. [32]Leah conceived and bore a son, and she named him Reuben; for she said, "It means, 'The LORD saw my misery; surely now my husband will love me.'" [33]She conceived again and bore a son, and said, "It means, 'The LORD heard that I was unloved,' and therefore he has given me this one also"; so she named him Simeon. [34]Again she conceived and bore a son, and she said, "Now at last my husband will become attached to me, since I have now borne him three sons"; that is why she named him Levi. [35]Once more she conceived and bore a son, and she said, "This time I will give thanks to the LORD"; therefore she named him Judah. Then she stopped bearing children.

continue

CHAPTER 30

¹When Rachel saw that she had not borne children to Jacob, she became envious of her sister. She said to Jacob, "Give me children or I shall die!" ²Jacob became angry with Rachel and said, "Can I take the place of God, who has denied you the fruit of the womb?" ³She replied, "Here is my maidservant Bilhah. Have intercourse with her, and let her give birth on my knees, so that I too may have children through her." ⁴So she gave him her maidservant Bilhah as wife, and Jacob had intercourse with her. ⁵When Bilhah conceived and bore a son for Jacob, ⁶Rachel said, "God has vindicated me; indeed he has heeded my plea and given me a son." Therefore she named him Dan. ⁷Rachel's maidservant Bilhah conceived again and bore a second son for Jacob, ⁸and Rachel said, "I have wrestled strenuously with my sister, and I have prevailed." So she named him Naphtali.

⁹When Leah saw that she had ceased to bear children, she took her maidservant Zilpah and gave her to Jacob as wife. ¹⁰So Leah's maidservant Zilpah bore a son for Jacob. ¹¹Leah then said, "What good luck!" So she named him Gad. ¹²Then Leah's maidservant Zilpah bore a second son to Jacob; ¹³and Leah said, "What good fortune, because women will call me fortunate!" So she named him Asher.

¹⁴One day, during the wheat harvest, Reuben went out and came upon some mandrakes in the field which he brought home to his mother Leah. Rachel said to Leah, "Please give me some of your son's mandrakes." ¹⁵Leah replied, "Was it not enough for you to take away my husband, that you must now take my son's mandrakes too?" Rachel answered, "In that case Jacob may lie with you tonight in exchange for your son's mandrakes." ¹⁶That evening, when Jacob came in from the field, Leah went out to meet him. She said, "You must have intercourse with me, because I have hired you with my son's mandrakes." So that night he lay with her, ¹⁷and God listened to Leah; she conceived and bore a fifth son to Jacob. ¹⁸Leah

continue

then reports that she also bears a daughter whom she names Dinah. No interpretation of her name or other details are given about Dinah.

Only after Jacob already has ten sons and a daughter does Rachel bear a son (v. 22). The narrative specifies that God remembers her; that is, God focuses attention on her. She bears Joseph, whose name suggests both removing her past shame and adding hope and joy to her future. By now eleven sons are born to Jacob and his four women: six to Leah, two to each of the two maids Bilhah and Zilpah, and one to Rachel. In addition he has one daughter by Leah. Throughout the narrative, all the women compete with one another for Jacob's love and for children. While the humans strive to control the situation, the narrative repeats frequently that it is God who gives children, assuring that the promise of descendants moves forward into the next generation.

then said, "God has given me my wages for giving my maidservant to my husband"; so she named him Issachar. [19]Leah conceived again and bore a sixth son to Jacob; [20]and Leah said, "God has brought me a precious gift. This time my husband will honor me, because I have borne him six sons"; so she named him Zebulun. [21]Afterwards she gave birth to a daughter, and she named her Dinah.

[22]Then God remembered Rachel. God listened to her and made her fruitful. [23]She conceived and bore a son, and she said, "God has removed my disgrace." [24]She named him Joseph, saying, "May the LORD add another son for me!"

EXPLORING LESSON ONE

1. What is divinely revealed to Rebekah about her difficult pregnancy (25:23)?

_____

_____

_____

_____

2. What problems do you see with parental favoritism of one child over another (25:28)?

_____

_____

_____

_____

3. If you have felt taken advantage of by a family member or close friend (25:27-34), how have you moved beyond this situation into forgiveness?

_____

_____

_____

_____

_____

4. What does Isaac's blessing promise to Jacob (27:27-29)?

_____

_____

_____

_____

5. Why might the story of Isaac, Rebekah, and Abimelech (26:1-31) seem familiar to readers of earlier sections of Genesis? (See 20:1-18; 21:22-34.)

_____

_____

_____

_____

_____

6. Jacob has a special dream during his journey to his Uncle Laban's (28:10-22). Describe a dream that has carried special meaning in your own life. Consider your deepest desires as a form of dreams also.

_____

_____

_____

_____

7. In Genesis 28:16, Jacob realizes God's presence only in hindsight. When has such a realization happened to you?

_____

_____

_____

_____

8. Why does Jacob's plan to marry Rachel (29:14-30) prove to be more difficult to achieve than Abraham's earlier plan to win a wife for Isaac (24:1-67)?

_____

_____

_____

_____

9. How does Laban prove to be as deceitful as Jacob (29:14b-30)? (See 27:1-29.)

_____

_____

_____

_____

10. Read the account describing the birth of Jacob's children (29:31–30:24). How does this account highlight the role of God in their family's growth?

_____

_____

_____

_____

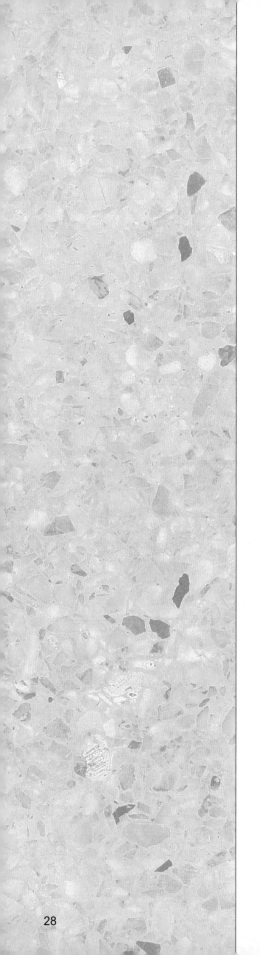

CLOSING PRAYER

Prayer

"Truly, the Lord is in this place and I did not know it!" (Gen 28:16)

You are the God of surprises, coming to us in the most ordinary of places and through events that have the power to draw us to you. Gift us with the wisdom of awareness and wonder in your presence. This day we offer thanksgiving, especially for . . .

LESSON TWO

Genesis 30:25–34:31

Begin your personal study and group discussion with a simple and sincere prayer such as:

Prayer

God of my ancestors in faith, open my eyes and ears and heart as I reflect on these people whom you called centuries ago.

Read the Bible text of Genesis 30:25–34:31 found in the outside columns of pages 30–39, highlighting what stands out to you.

Read the accompanying commentary to add to your understanding.

Respond to the questions on pages 40–41, Exploring Lesson Two.

The Closing Prayer on page 42 is for your personal use and may be used at the end of group discussion.

Jacob Outwits Laban

²⁵After Rachel gave birth to Joseph, Jacob said to Laban: "Allow me to go to my own region and land. ²⁶Give me my wives and my children for whom I served you and let me go, for you know the service that I rendered you." ²⁷Laban answered him: "If you will please! I have learned through divination that the Lᴏʀᴅ has blessed me because of you." ²⁸He continued, "State the wages I owe you, and I will pay them." ²⁹Jacob replied: "You know what work I did for you and how well your livestock fared under my care; ³⁰the little you had before I came has grown into an abundance, since the Lᴏʀᴅ has blessed you in my company. Now, when can I do something for my own household as well?" ³¹Laban asked, "What should I give you?" Jacob answered: "You do not have to give me anything. If you do this thing for me, I will again pasture and tend your sheep. ³²Let me go through your whole flock today and remove from it every dark animal among the lambs and every spotted or speckled one among the goats. These will be my wages. ³³In the future, whenever you check on my wages, my honesty will testify for me: any animal that is not speckled or spotted among the goats, or dark among the lambs, got into my possession by theft!" ³⁴Laban said, "Very well. Let it be as you say."

³⁵That same day Laban removed the streaked and spotted he-goats and all the speckled and spotted she-goats, all those with some white on them, as well as every dark lamb, and he put them in the care of his sons. ³⁶Then he put a three days' journey between himself and Jacob, while Jacob was pasturing the rest of Laban's flock.

³⁷Jacob, however, got some fresh shoots of poplar, almond and plane trees, and he peeled white stripes in them by laying bare the white core of the shoots. ³⁸The shoots that he had peeled he then set upright in the watering troughs where the animals came to drink, so that they would be in front of them. When the animals were in heat as they came to drink, ³⁹the goats mated by the shoots,

continue

30:25-43 Jacob tricks Laban

The story shifts back to the relationship between Jacob and his father-in-law Laban, and continues the motif of trickery that permeates the story of Jacob's marriage, his wives, and his children. After fourteen years of working for Laban in exchange for his two wives, he works for Laban six more years. By the end of the twenty years he has twelve children. In accordance with the divine promise to Jacob in his dream at Bethel to bring him back to his father's land (28:15), Jacob asks Laban's permission to return home. The history of trickery between the two men leads us to suspect that the leave-taking will not be a simple one. They bargain for a fair arrangement: Laban realizes he will lose the valuable services of his son-in-law, who has been a blessing to him; and Jacob wants compensation for all his labor.

Jacob requests some of the animals from Laban's flocks: he asks for the dark sheep and the spotted goats. These animals, a small proportion of Laban's flocks, do not have the usual coloring. The arrangement will, however, be a foolproof way to determine which animals belong to which of the men. Laban separates the flocks according to color as agreed, and puts his sons in charge of those flocks destined for Jacob. Jacob alludes to their history of trickery when he asserts his honesty to Laban in verse

33. Laban moves his flocks a three-day journey away, but Jacob takes advantage of the isolation of those flocks to breed animals selectively, thus increasing the size and quality of his own flocks and other holdings (v. 43). Eventually he justifies this practice by attributing the idea to a dream (31:10-13), thus intimating that it is God's plan.

Jacob's scheme is so successful that he arouses the suspicion and mistrust of Laban and his sons. The time to depart has arrived, and once again we expect complications.

31:1-54 Jacob takes leave of Laban

After the payment for Jacob's services is settled and Jacob's continued presence with his uncle has become very problematic, Jacob receives word from the Lord to return home with the assurance of divine protection. But several more complications arise before the men finally separate. The plot reflects the duplicity, not only of Jacob and Laban, but also of Rachel. The episode takes place in five stages.

In the first, verses 1-16, Jacob sends for his two wives and explains that the Lord has instructed him to leave Laban and return to his own land in fulfillment of the agreement made at Bethel. He gives a detailed description of the situation, putting his own actions in a good light and Laban's in a bad light. Both wives agree with Jacob that their father has been unfair in dealing, not only with Jacob, but also with them. It is unusual that the two are of one mind; their agreement expresses their bitterness at their father's treatment of them. They encourage Jacob to do as God instructs.

In the second, verses 17-21, the family flees. They depart while Laban is away, taking with them all Jacob acquired over the years. In addition, Rachel steals her father's household gods. The reason for the theft is not clear: perhaps she wants simply to deprive him of them, or perhaps to use them for her own benefit, either by claiming them as an inheritance or by using them for religious purposes. In 27:43 Rebekah insisted that Jacob flee from his father's house; now he flees from his father-in-law's house.

and so they gave birth to streaked, speckled and spotted young. [40]The sheep, on the other hand, Jacob kept apart, and he made these animals face the streaked or completely dark animals of Laban. Thus he produced flocks of his own, which he did not put with Laban's flock. [41]Whenever the hardier animals were in heat, Jacob would set the shoots in the troughs in full view of these animals, so that they mated by the shoots; [42]but with the weaker animals he would not put the shoots there. So the feeble animals would go to Laban, but the hardy ones to Jacob. [43]So the man grew exceedingly prosperous, and he owned large flocks, male and female servants, camels, and donkeys.

CHAPTER 31

Flight from Laban

[1]Jacob heard that Laban's sons were saying, "Jacob has taken everything that belonged to our father, and he has produced all this wealth from our father's property." [2]Jacob perceived, too, that Laban's attitude toward him was not what it had previously been. [3]Then the LORD said to Jacob: Return to the land of your ancestors, where you were born, and I will be with you.

[4]So Jacob sent for Rachel and Leah to meet him in the field where his flock was. [5]There he said to them: "I have noticed that your father's attitude toward me is not as it was in the past; but the God of my father has been with me. [6]You know well that with all my strength I served your father; [7]yet your father cheated me and changed my wages ten times. God, however, did not let him do me any harm. [8]Whenever your father said, 'The speckled animals will be your wages,' the entire flock would bear speckled young; whenever he said, 'The streaked animals will be your wages,' the entire flock would bear streaked young. [9]So God took away your father's livestock and gave it to me. [10]Once, during the flock's mating season, I had a dream in which I saw he-goats mating that were streaked, speckled and mottled. [11]In the

continue

dream God's angel said to me, 'Jacob!' and I replied, 'Here I am!' ¹²Then he said: 'Look up and see. All the he-goats that are mating are streaked, speckled and mottled, for I have seen all the things that Laban has been doing to you. ¹³I am the God of Bethel, where you anointed a sacred pillar and made a vow to me. Get up now! Leave this land and return to the land of your birth.'"

¹⁴Rachel and Leah answered him: "Do we still have an heir's portion in our father's house? ¹⁵Are we not regarded by him as outsiders? He not only sold us; he has even used up the money that he got for us! ¹⁶All the wealth that God took away from our father really belongs to us and our children. So do whatever God has told you." ¹⁷Jacob proceeded to put his children and wives on camels, ¹⁸and he drove off all his livestock and all the property he had acquired in Paddan-aram, to go to his father Isaac in the land of Canaan.

¹⁹Now Laban was away shearing his sheep, and Rachel had stolen her father's household images. ²⁰Jacob had hoodwinked Laban the Aramean by not telling him that he was going to flee. ²¹Thus he fled with all that he had. Once he was across the Euphrates, he headed for the hill country of Gilead.

²²On the third day, word came to Laban that Jacob had fled. ²³Taking his kinsmen with him, he pursued him for seven days until he caught up with him in the hill country of Gilead. ²⁴But that night God appeared to Laban the Aramean in a dream and said to him: Take care not to say anything to Jacob.

Jacob and Laban in Gilead

²⁵When Laban overtook Jacob, Jacob's tents were pitched in the hill country; Laban also pitched his tents in the hill country of Gilead. ²⁶Laban said to Jacob, "How could you hoodwink me and carry off my daughters like prisoners of war? ²⁷Why did you dupe me by stealing away secretly? You did not tell me! I would have sent you off with joyful singing to the sound of tambourines and harps. ²⁸You did not even allow me a parting kiss to my daughters and grandchildren! Now what you have done makes no sense. ²⁹I have it in my power to harm all of you; but last night the God of your father said to me, 'Take care not to say anything to Jacob!' ³⁰Granted that you had to leave because you were longing for your father's house, why did you steal my gods?" ³¹Jacob replied to Laban, "I was frightened at the thought that you might take your daughters away from me by force. ³²As for your gods, the one you find them with shall not remain alive! If, with our kinsmen looking on, you identify anything here as belonging to you, take it." Jacob had no idea that Rachel had stolen the household images.

³³Laban then went in and searched Jacob's tent and Leah's tent, as well as the tents of the two maidservants; but he did not find them. Leaving Leah's tent, he went into Rachel's. ³⁴Meanwhile Rachel had taken the household images, put them inside the camel's saddlebag, and seated herself upon them. When Laban had rummaged through her whole tent without finding them, ³⁵she said to her father, "Do not let my lord be angry that I cannot rise in your presence; I am having my period." So, despite his search, he did not find the household images.

³⁶Jacob, now angered, confronted Laban and demanded, "What crime or offense have I committed that you should hound me? ³⁷Now that you have rummaged through all my things, what have you found from your household belongings? Produce it here before your kinsmen and mine, and let them decide between the two of us.

³⁸"In the twenty years that I was under you, no ewe or she-goat of yours ever miscarried, and I have never eaten rams of your flock. ³⁹I never brought you an animal torn by wild beasts; I made good the loss myself. You held me responsible for anything stolen by day or night. ⁴⁰Often the scorching heat devoured me by day, and the frost by night, while sleep fled from my eyes! ⁴¹Of the

continue

In the third, verses 22-35, Laban learns that the party has fled and sets out in pursuit. After seven days, as he nears the fugitives, he has a dream warning him not to interfere with Jacob. He confronts his son-in-law, accusing him of deceit and kidnapping. He bemoans his lost opportunity to give a proper farewell to his daughters and grandchildren, and then refers to the stolen household gods. Laban's complaint is filled with irony in light of his own treatment of Jacob from the time they first met. Jacob knows nothing of the stolen household gods, and assures Laban that he may have anything he finds that belongs to him.

Laban immediately begins to search the tents of each member of the party, saving Rachel's until last. She is ready for him: she had hidden the statues in a camel cushion, a combination saddle and storage box that is placed on a camel to provide seating and storage for the rider. She sits on the camel cushion, and protests that she cannot get up because she is menstruating. This adds to the irony of the situation: Rachel will not stand up to allow her father to search for the idols; in fact, he ought not to be in her presence under pain of defilement (Lev 15:19-23); but she defiles the idols by sitting on them in her claimed state of ritual uncleanness while at the same time protecting them from harm. Her action suggests that she herself does not believe the statues possess any power; otherwise she would treat them with respect. She accomplishes her purpose, however: Laban gives up his search for the idols. She also demonstrates that she is as capable of trickery as her husband and her father.

In the fourth stage, verses 36-42, Jacob takes the offensive, rehearsing all the injustices he has suffered at Laban's hands since his arrival at his home twenty years ago.

In the fifth stage, verses 43-54, Laban proposes that the two of them make an agreement. This will assure him that his family will be safe in Jacob's care, and that the two families will not interfere with each other but will live in peaceful coexistence. They formalize the agreement by erecting a stone pillar and then sharing

twenty years that I have now spent in your household, I served you fourteen years for your two daughters and six years for your flock, while you changed my wages ten times. [42]If the God of my father, the God of Abraham and the Fear of Isaac, had not been on my side, you would now have sent me away empty-handed. But God saw my plight and the fruits of my toil, and last night he reproached you."

[43]Laban replied to Jacob: "The daughters are mine, their children are mine, and the flocks are mine; everything you see belongs to me. What can I do now for my own daughters and for the children they have borne? [44]Come, now, let us make a covenant, you and I; and it will be a treaty between you and me."

[45]Then Jacob took a stone and set it up as a sacred pillar. [46]Jacob said to his kinsmen, "Gather stones." So they got stones and made a mound; and they ate there at the mound. [47]Laban called it Jegar-sahadutha, but Jacob called it Galeed. [48]Laban said, "This mound will be a witness from now on between you and me." That is why it was named Galeed— [49]and also Mizpah, for he said: "May the LORD keep watch between you and me when we are out of each other's sight. [50]If you mistreat my daughters, or take other wives besides my daughters, know that even though no one else is there, God will be a witness between you and me."

[51]Laban said further to Jacob: "Here is this mound, and here is the sacred pillar that I have set up between you and me. [52]This mound will be a witness, and this sacred pillar will be a witness, that, with hostile intent, I may not pass beyond this mound into your territory, nor may you pass beyond it into mine. [53]May the God of Abraham and the God of Nahor, the God of their father, judge between us!" Jacob took the oath by the Fear of his father Isaac. [54]He then offered a sacrifice on the mountain and invited his kinsmen to share in the meal. When they had eaten, they passed the night on the mountain.

continue

CHAPTER 32

¹Early the next morning, Laban kissed his grandchildren and his daughters and blessed them; then he set out on his journey back home. ²Meanwhile Jacob continued on his own way, and God's angels encountered him. ³When Jacob saw them he said, "This is God's encampment." So he named that place Mahanaim.

Envoys to Esau

⁴Jacob sent messengers ahead to his brother Esau in the land of Seir, the country of Edom, ⁵ordering them: "Thus you shall say to my lord Esau: 'Thus says your servant Jacob: I have been residing with Laban and have been delayed until now. ⁶I own oxen, donkeys and sheep, as well as male and female servants. I have sent my lord this message in the hope of gaining your favor.'" ⁷When the messengers returned to Jacob, they said, "We found your brother Esau. He is now coming to meet you, and four hundred men are with him."

⁸Jacob was very much frightened. In his anxiety, he divided the people who were with him, as well as his flocks, herds and camels, into two camps. ⁹"If Esau should come and attack one camp," he reasoned, "the remaining camp may still escape." ¹⁰Then Jacob prayed: "God of my father Abraham and God of my father Isaac! You, LORD, who said to me, 'Go back to your land and your relatives, and I will be good to you.' ¹¹I am unworthy of all the acts of kindness and faithfulness that you have performed for your servant: although I crossed the Jordan here with nothing but my staff, I have now grown into two camps. ¹²Save me from the hand of my brother, from the hand of Esau! Otherwise I fear that he will come and strike me down and the mothers with the children. ¹³You yourself said, 'I will be very good to you, and I will make your descendants like the sands of the sea, which are too numerous to count.'"

¹⁴After passing the night there, Jacob selected from what he had with him a present for his

continue

a meal. This meal probably includes only the two men, as Jacob then invites his men to share the meal in verse 54, after he offers a sacrifice. Both men give a name to the place, each in his own native language, further highlighting the separation that is taking place between the two families. Laban invokes the God of Abraham and the God of Nahor, the ancestral deities of both families. Jacob invokes his father's name, offers a sacrifice, and invites his men to the sacrificial meal to finalize the treaty.

32:1-3 The final leave-taking

Both parties spend the night in proximity to each other, and then Laban bids his family farewell and the two parties separate. This final scene is stark in its simplicity after the many duplicitous actions throughout Jacob's stay with Laban. As Jacob begins his journey homeward, angels appear, just as they did when he first left his parents' home at the beginning of his journey to Haran (28:12). While they do not take an active part in events, they mark the stages of Jacob's journey and the presence of God with Jacob in his travels.

32:4–33:20 The meeting of Jacob and Esau

When Jacob sets out, his first project is to make contact with his brother Esau. Jacob fled from his parents' home after he usurped the blessing intended for Esau, and Esau vowed to kill him (27:41). Now he returns home with a large family, and must protect both them and himself from harm. His honor as head of his family and also his promise to Laban demand that he take whatever steps are necessary toward this end.

Verses 4-22 describe four steps he takes in preparation for meeting his brother. First, he sends messengers with a conciliatory word to Esau, who sends word in return that he and his army will meet Jacob. Next, fearing for the safety of himself and his family, he divides his party into two groups. That way, if harm comes to one, the other will be spared. Then he prays to the God of his ancestors for help, recalling the promises God made to him when he started out from home (28:13-15) and when he began his journey home from Haran (31:3). Fearing what his brother might do to him and his family, he reminds God of the divine promise of descendants. His prayer calls on God's faithfulness rather than any claim of his own to divine care. Finally, he selects an extravagant number of livestock to give to his brother, and sends them ahead in droves, each in the care of one of his servants. After making all these preparations, he sends his family across the Jabbok, and he stays behind for the night. Crossing the Jabbok marks the family's entry into Jacob's homeland.

Verses 23-33 give a vague description of a curious incident: an unidentified man wrestles with Jacob until dawn. The narrative does not identify the person or give information about where he came from or how he happened to find Jacob until the end of the incident. When the stranger realizes he cannot defeat Jacob he injures his hip, leaving Jacob with a limp. Then the man asks to be released, suggesting that Jacob the heel-grabber has him in his grasp. Jacob agrees on condition that the man bless him. He gives Jacob the new name of Israel, but refuses to tell Jacob his own name, and then disappears as mysteriously as he came. The name Jacob gives to the place, Peniel, lets us know that his assailant is God. This mysterious episode describes a universal human experience of passing a restless night wrestling out a dilemma. By the time the sun rises Jacob has faced down the enemy and has come to a new awareness that God is with him. A brief etiological note follows, connecting Jacob's hip injury with the custom of not eating the sciatic nerve. Here for the first time the narrative uses the term "Israelites" in honor of Jacob's new name; it appears frequently throughout the Old Testament.

After all the preparations including Jacob's night of wrestling with the angel, the brothers meet in 33:1-20. The meeting is affectionate, respectful, yet guarded. When Jacob sees his brother coming with his four hundred men, he arranges his wives and their maids with their respective children, in order of importance and affection. Jacob's bow repeats Abraham's gesture when he received the three visitors in 18:2.

brother Esau: [15]two hundred she-goats and twenty he-goats; two hundred ewes and twenty rams; [16]thirty female camels and their young; forty cows and ten bulls; twenty female donkeys and ten male donkeys. [17]He put these animals in the care of his servants, in separate herds, and he told the servants, "Go on ahead of me, but keep some space between the herds." [18]He ordered the servant in the lead, "When my brother Esau meets you and asks, 'To whom do you belong? Where are you going? To whom do these animals ahead of you belong?' [19]tell him, 'To your servant Jacob, but they have been sent as a gift to my lord Esau. Jacob himself is right behind us.'" [20]He also ordered the second servant and the third and all the others who followed behind the herds: "Thus and so you shall say to Esau, when you reach him; [21]and also tell him, 'Your servant Jacob is right behind us.'" For Jacob reasoned, "If I first appease him with a gift that precedes me, then later, when I face him, perhaps he will forgive me." [22]So the gifts went on ahead of him, while he stayed that night in the camp.

Jacob's New Name

[23]That night, however, Jacob arose, took his two wives, with the two maidservants and his eleven children, and crossed the ford of the Jabbok. [24]After he got them and brought them across the wadi and brought over what belonged to him, [25]Jacob was left there alone. Then a man wrestled with him until the break of dawn. [26]When the man saw that he could not prevail over him, he struck Jacob's hip at its socket, so that Jacob's socket was dislocated as he wrestled with him. [27]The man then said, "Let me go, for it is daybreak." But Jacob said, "I will not let you go until you bless me." [28]"What is your name?" the man asked. He answered, "Jacob." [29]Then the man said, "You shall no longer be named Jacob, but Israel, because you have contended with divine and human beings and have prevailed." [30]Jacob then asked him, "Please tell me your name." He answered, "Why do you ask for my name?" With

continue

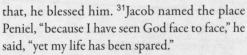

that, he blessed him. ³¹Jacob named the place Peniel, "because I have seen God face to face," he said, "yet my life has been spared."

³²At sunrise, as he left Penuel, Jacob limped along because of his hip. ³³That is why, to this day, the Israelites do not eat the sciatic muscle that is on the hip socket, because he had struck Jacob's hip socket at the sciatic muscle.

CHAPTER 33

Jacob and Esau Meet

¹Jacob looked up and saw Esau coming, and with him four hundred men. So he divided his children among Leah, Rachel, and the two maidservants, ²putting the maidservants and their children first, Leah and her children next, and Rachel and Joseph last. ³He himself went on ahead of them, bowing to the ground seven times, until he reached his brother. ⁴Esau ran to meet him, embraced him, and flinging himself on his neck, kissed him as he wept.

⁵Then Esau looked up and saw the women and children and asked, "Who are these with you?" Jacob answered, "They are the children with whom God has graciously favored your servant." ⁶Then the maidservants and their children came forward and bowed low; ⁷next, Leah and her children came forward and bowed low; lastly, Joseph and Rachel came forward and bowed low. ⁸Then Esau asked, "What did you intend with all those herds that I encountered?" Jacob answered, "It was to gain my lord's favor." ⁹Esau replied, "I have plenty; my brother, you should keep what is yours." ¹⁰"No, I beg you!" said Jacob. "If you will do me the favor, accept this gift from me, since to see your face is for me like seeing the face of God—and you have received me so kindly. ¹¹Accept the gift I have brought you. For God has been generous toward me, and I have an abundance." Since he urged him strongly, Esau accepted.

¹²Then Esau said, "Let us break camp and be on our way; I will travel in front of you." ¹³But Jacob replied: "As my lord knows, the children are

continue

It is also ironic in light of the divine words to Rebekah when the twins were still in the womb (25:23) and Isaac's blessing of Jacob in 27:29. Esau's tender, affectionate greeting reverses the kiss Isaac gave Jacob when Jacob stole Esau's blessing.

After their greeting the conversation becomes cautious when Esau inquires about all the gifts Jacob has brought. He demurs, perhaps according to custom, perhaps in an effort not to be beholden to his brother. Jacob remains respectful and deferential, and makes a connection between seeing Esau and encountering his assailant the previous night when he refers to the face of God. Esau accepts Jacob's gifts but does not offer any in return: Jacob's gifts are restitution for past wrongs rather than fraternal offerings.

The brothers arrange to continue their travels, negotiating whether to journey together or separately. The narrative suggests hesitancy on Jacob's part when he prefers to travel apart from Esau's men. In fact, Jacob does not follow Esau as he said he would, but goes in the opposite direction and establishes a temporary home for his family. The brothers leave each other on that somewhat wary note.

Jacob and his family stay temporarily at Succoth, then continue on to Shechem where the Lord appeared to Abraham when he first came into the land (12:6). There Jacob purchases land from the Shechemites and builds an altar to the God of Israel, his new name. This is the second purchase of land recorded in Genesis; the first is the burial place for Sarah. The narrative does not specify the purpose for which this purchase will be used; it seems to represent Jacob's belief that God will continue to care for him and his family in their new home. But the following chapters show that Jacob's hope of peaceful settlement in the land is mistaken.

 Is there someone with whom you need to be reconciled? Envision a **bridge of trust** between your hearts. In memory of Jacob and Esau, come to meet that person on a pathway carved out of trust. Stand together and experience the presence of God.

34:1-31 Dinah among the Shechemites

The narrative then focuses on Dinah, who goes out to meet her new neighbors. By specifying that she is Leah's daughter the narrative casts her in a negative light. Her action has been interpreted in both positive and negative ways: either she is innocently exploring her new neighborhood or looking for companionship, or she acts inappropriately in going among Canaanites or leaving the family compound (see 24:3, 37). Perhaps the ambiguity of the statement leaves open all the above possibilities. She goes out to see the women, and is seen by the son of the chief, Hamor. She goes out as an active young woman and immediately becomes a passive victim. Things happen quickly, as the rapid succession of verbs indicates. The actions that follow are equally startling because of the abrupt shift they express.

In verse 5 the scene shifts to Dinah's father Jacob, who hears about the incident but decides against taking any action because his sons are working in the fields. This is an odd stance for Jacob, who usually takes matters in hand and finds ways to deal with complicated situations. Jacob apparently sends for his sons, who arrive to find Shechem's father Hamor making his request to their father. The brothers react with indignation to what Shechem has done: he did not simply violate Dinah and her entire family, but violated the moral climate of the community.

Several aspects of the narrative are complicated by layers of editing within the text. From a legal perspective Dinah's family is entitled to the bride-price for a virgin, but because Jacob is a resident alien, his claim to restitution is unclear. The relevant law in Exodus 22:15-16 reflects a time later than the ancestral period. In addition, the second half of verse 7 judges Shechem's sin in language typical of the monarchic period rather than the time of the ancestors.

In verse 8 Hamor ignores the moral question and focuses on the political and economic benefit to Jacob's family if Dinah is given to Shechem in marriage. Shechem then enters the conversation and offers to give whatever is

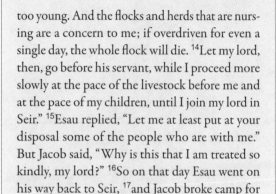

too young. And the flocks and herds that are nursing are a concern to me; if overdriven for even a single day, the whole flock will die. ¹⁴Let my lord, then, go before his servant, while I proceed more slowly at the pace of the livestock before me and at the pace of my children, until I join my lord in Seir." ¹⁵Esau replied, "Let me at least put at your disposal some of the people who are with me." But Jacob said, "Why is this that I am treated so kindly, my lord?" ¹⁶So on that day Esau went on his way back to Seir, ¹⁷and Jacob broke camp for Succoth. There Jacob built a home for himself and made booths for his livestock. That is why the place was named Succoth.

¹⁸Jacob arrived safely at the city of Shechem, which is in the land of Canaan, when he came from Paddan-aram. He encamped in sight of the city. ¹⁹The plot of ground on which he had pitched his tent he bought for a hundred pieces of money from the descendants of Hamor, the father of Shechem. ²⁰He set up an altar there and invoked "El, the God of Israel."

CHAPTER 34

The Rape of Dinah

¹Dinah, the daughter whom Leah had borne to Jacob, went out to visit some of the women of the land. ²When Shechem, son of Hamor the Hivite, the leader of the region, saw her, he seized her and lay with her by force. ³He was strongly attracted to Dinah, daughter of Jacob, and was in love with the young woman. So he spoke affectionately to her. ⁴Shechem said to his father Hamor, "Get me this young woman for a wife."

⁵Meanwhile, Jacob heard that Shechem had defiled his daughter Dinah; but since his sons were out in the field with his livestock, Jacob kept quiet until they came home. ⁶Now Hamor, the father of Shechem, went out to discuss the matter with Jacob, ⁷just as Jacob's sons were coming in from the field. When they heard the news, the men were indignant and extremely angry. Shechem had committed an outrage in Israel by lying with Jacob's

continue

daughter; such a thing is not done. ⁸Hamor appealed to them, saying: "My son Shechem has his heart set on your daughter. Please give her to him as a wife. ⁹Intermarry with us; give your daughters to us, and take our daughters for yourselves. ¹⁰Thus you can live among us. The land is open before you. Settle and move about freely in it and acquire holdings here." ¹¹Then Shechem appealed to Dinah's father and brothers: "Do me this favor, and whatever you ask from me, I will give. ¹²No matter how high you set the bridal price and gift, I will give you whatever you ask from me; only give me the young woman as a wife."

Revenge of Jacob's Sons

¹³Jacob's sons replied to Shechem and his father Hamor with guile, speaking as they did because he had defiled their sister Dinah. ¹⁴They said to them, "We are not able to do this thing: to give our sister to an uncircumcised man. For that would be a disgrace for us. ¹⁵Only on this condition will we agree to that: that you become like us by having every male among you circumcised. ¹⁶Then we will give you our daughters and take your daughters in marriage; we will settle among you and become one people. ¹⁷But if you do not listen to us and be circumcised, we will take our daughter and go."

¹⁸Their proposal pleased Hamor and his son Shechem. ¹⁹The young man lost no time in acting on the proposal, since he wanted Jacob's daughter. Now he was more highly regarded than anyone else in his father's house. ²⁰So Hamor and his son Shechem went to the gate of their city and said to the men of their city: ²¹"These men are friendly toward us. Let them settle in the land and move about in it freely; there is ample room in the land for them. We can take their daughters in marriage and give our daughters to them. ²²But only on this condition will the men agree to live with us and form one people with us: that every male among us be circumcised as they themselves are. ²³Would not their livestock, their property, and all their

continue

appropriate, apparently acknowledging that his defilement of Dinah requires some sort of restitution.

Jacob's sons outwardly maintain their focus on the religious and ethical dimension of the situation; they object to their sister marrying an uncircumcised man. Only if all the Shechemite males agree to be circumcised can Dinah's brothers agree to the marriage. In fact, in making this assertion they show themselves as capable of deception as their father (v. 13). Their intent is not to observe the religious custom; it is rather to set a trap for the men of Shechem.

Hamor and Shechem agree immediately to the brothers' request. One wonders if they realize the implications of the request: do they see it as a religious act? a political bargain? a ruse? The narrative does not specify. We suspect they anticipate the economic gain because, when they urge the men of the city to comply, they add a detail that is unknown to Dinah's brothers: the people of Shechem will then possess the livestock that belong to Jacob's family. The men of the city readily agree to the procedure.

The loyalty among Dinah and her full brothers is evident in their next move. While the men are recuperating from the procedure, and are in great pain, two of her full brothers (that is, the sons of Leah), Simeon and Levi, kill all the males including Hamor and Shechem, then take Dinah from Shechem's house. Again the text leaves us wondering: is this a forceful removal or a rescue? Is Dinah eager to leave or reluctant? The text does not specify. Then Jacob's other sons completely sack the city and take the spoils for themselves.

Jacob finally takes a stand in verse 30, chastising Simeon and Levi for destroying Shechem. (Jacob's deathbed curse of these two sons in 49:5-7 reflects his outraged response to this destruction.) His response is startling: Jacob reprimands the two sons who come to Dinah's rescue, after he seems to have chosen not to make an issue of the terrible violation to her and to the entire family. Now that he has purchased a piece of land in the area, he hopes to live there in peace with the neighboring people who greatly outnumber them. He thinks of the number of his men, small in comparison to his neighbors. The brothers think of avenging the outrage to their sister and their entire family. Their final question summarizes the ambivalence and lack of resolution between father and sons and between competing values as the family settles in the land. Family concerns must be weighed in relation to relations with neighbors, and there are no easy answers.

animals then be ours? Let us just agree with them, so that they will settle among us."

²⁴All who went out of the gate of the city listened to Hamor and his son Shechem, and all the males, all those who went out of the gate of the city, were circumcised. ²⁵On the third day, while they were still in pain, two of Jacob's sons, Simeon and Levi, brothers of Dinah, each took his sword, advanced against the unsuspecting city and massacred all the males. ²⁶After they had killed Hamor and his son Shechem with the sword, they took Dinah from Shechem's house and left. ²⁷Then the other sons of Jacob followed up the slaughter and sacked the city because their sister had been defiled. ²⁸They took their sheep, cattle and donkeys, whatever was in the city and in the surrounding country. ²⁹They carried off all their wealth, their children, and their women, and looted whatever was in the houses.

³⁰Jacob said to Simeon and Levi: "You have brought trouble upon me by making me repugnant to the inhabitants of the land, the Canaanites and the Perizzites. I have so few men that, if these people unite against me and attack me, I and my household will be wiped out." ³¹But they retorted, "Should our sister be treated like a prostitute?"

EXPLORING LESSON TWO

1. How do Laban (30:35-36), Jacob (30:37-43), and Rachel (31:33-35) each show their deviousness toward other members of their family?

_____

_____

_____

_____

2. What are the terms of the covenant that Jacob and Laban make with each other (31:43-54)?

_____

_____

_____

_____

3. What do you think creates good relationships with in-laws (31:43-54)? (See Ruth 1; Tobit 10:12; 14:13.)

_____

_____

_____

_____

4. Why is Jacob so afraid of his brother Esau (32:4-7)? (See 25:29-34; 27:1-45.)

_____

_____

_____

_____

5. When Jacob prepares to meet Esau, what does he do that demonstrates he still has favorites among his family (32:8-9; 33:1-2)?

_____

_____

_____

_____

6. What is ironic about the manner in which Jacob approaches Esau (33:1-4)? (See 25:22-23; 27:29.)

_____

_____

_____

_____

_____

7. What evidence is there that Jacob might still fear Esau even after they have been reconciled (33:12-20)?

_____

_____

_____

_____

_____

8. How are Jacob's sons able to deceive the Shechemites (34:1-26)?

_____

_____

_____

_____

_____

9. a) What does Jacob warn his sons will be the result of their murderous actions (34:30-31)?

_____

_____

_____

_____

   b) When disastrous results follow acts of revenge or deception, what lessons can we learn? (See Deut 32:35; Matt 5:39: Rom 12:19.)

_____

_____

_____

_____

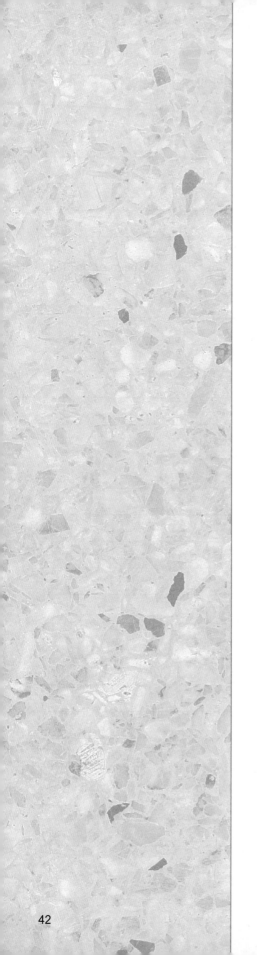

CLOSING PRAYER

Prayer

"If you will do me the favor, accept this gift from me, since to see you is for me like seeing the face of God . . ." (Gen 33:10)

You, God, revealed yourself in the reconciliation of two brothers, Esau and Jacob. Open us to your love that repairs broken relationships. Help us to see your face in our neighbor, be they friend or foe. This day we pray for healing between enemies, between countries at war, especially . . .

LESSON THREE

Genesis 35–39

Begin your personal study and group discussion with a simple and sincere prayer such as:

Prayer

God of my ancestors in faith, open my eyes and ears and heart as I reflect on these people whom you called centuries ago.

Read the Bible text of Genesis 35–39 found in the outside columns of pages 44–45, highlighting what stands out to you.

Read the accompanying commentary to add to your understanding.

Respond to the questions on pages 56–57, Exploring Lesson Three.

The Closing Prayer on page 58 is for your personal use and may be used at the end of group discussion.

CHAPTER 35

Bethel Revisited

¹God said to Jacob: Go up now to Bethel. Settle there and build an altar there to the God who appeared to you when you were fleeing from your brother Esau. ²So Jacob told his household and all who were with him: "Get rid of the foreign gods among you; then purify yourselves and change your clothes. ³Let us now go up to Bethel so that I might build an altar there to the God who answered me in the day of my distress and who has been with me wherever I have gone." ⁴They gave Jacob all the foreign gods in their possession and also the rings they had in their ears and Jacob buried them under the oak that is near Shechem. ⁵Then, as they set out, a great terror fell upon the surrounding towns, so that no one pursued the sons of Jacob.

⁶Thus Jacob and all the people who were with him arrived in Luz (now Bethel) in the land of Canaan. ⁷There he built an altar and called the place El-Bethel, for it was there that God had revealed himself to him when he was fleeing from his brother.

⁸Deborah, Rebekah's nurse, died. She was buried under the oak below Bethel, and so it was named Allon-bacuth.

⁹On Jacob's arrival from Paddan-aram, God appeared to him again and blessed him. ¹⁰God said to him:

Your name is Jacob.
You will no longer be named Jacob,
    but Israel will be your name.

So he was named Israel. ¹¹Then God said to him: I am God Almighty; be fruitful and multiply. A nation, indeed an assembly of nations, will stem from you, and kings will issue from your loins. ¹²The land I gave to Abraham and Isaac I will give to you; and to your descendants after you I will give the land.

¹³Then God departed from him. ¹⁴In the place where God had spoken with him, Jacob set up a

continue

35:1-29 Jacob settles in the land

Chapter 35 includes several episodes that seem at first glance to be isolated incidents in Jacob's life. In actuality each one relates to the whole cycle of stories about Jacob, showing that his life has come full circle during his absence from his father's house. The conniving, energetic youth who fled from his brother Esau has become a cautious father and protector of his land. This part of the narrative appears to be a compilation of stories from different sources; as a result we find incidents that appear to duplicate previous episodes. The chapter includes Jacob's visit to Bethel, the birth of his and Rachel's son Benjamin and the death of Rachel, Reuben's violation of Rachel's maid Bilhah, and the death and burial of Isaac.

After the massacre of the Shechemites, Jacob leaves that area at God's command and goes to Bethel. Jacob's threefold instruction depicts the preparations for departure as a liturgical act: he instructs them to dispose of their idols, purify themselves, and change clothes. Jacob follows the route taken by Abraham from Haran to Shechem and then to Bethel (12:4-8). The episode alludes to Jacob's night at Bethel when he fled from his brother Esau after stealing the blessing from their father (28:10-22). This time Jacob and his entire family are fleeing from the neighbors of the Shechemites. During his first stay at Bethel God promised to be with him in all his travels; now the family returns to the site to build an altar in thanks to God for fulfilling that promise. The people obey Jacob's three commands, and they set out on their journey of purification after the defilement of chapter 34. God continues to protect the travelers from the local people as they make their way to Bethel, where Jacob reiterates his earlier promise to honor God (28:19-22).

A very brief announcement of the death of Rebekah's nurse Deborah follows in verse 8, with the note that she is buried under a particular oak at Bethel. With her death Jacob's family relinquishes one of the few remaining ties with Laban and his land. Earlier they gave up another tie when Jacob buried their idols near Shechem (perhaps these were idols the family members brought with them from Haran, or perhaps they were part of the booty seized at Shechem).

In verse 9 the narrative relates another experience of Jacob at Bethel. God appears to him and gives him the name Israel; earlier the mysterious stranger gave him the name (32:29); here it comes directly from God. God also promises him descendants, a nation, and land in language similar to the promises to Abraham in 17:6-8, and to Jacob on his earlier visit (28:13-15). God specifies that these are the same promises given to his father and grandfather: now Jacob inherits them. Jacob sets up a stone pillar to mark the spot, blesses it, and names the place Bethel (see also 28:19). The similarities between this and earlier episodes suggest that they come from different sources; this version is associated with E.

Once again the family sets out and travels southward (v. 16). Rachel goes into very difficult labor and gives birth to a boy, thus bringing to fruition the name she gave Joseph when he was born: a prayer that the Lord would give her another son (30:24). Rachel's last act is to name her newborn son, characterizing him as the son of her distress. Jacob, however, gives him the name Benjamin ("Son of the Right Hand"). Rachel dies and is buried on the road to Bethlehem, where the narrator specifies that

sacred pillar, a stone pillar, and upon it he made a libation and poured out oil. [15]Jacob named the place where God spoke to him Bethel.

Jacob's Family

[16]Then they departed from Bethel; but while they still had some distance to go to Ephrath, Rachel went into labor and suffered great distress. [17]When her labor was most intense, the midwife said to her, "Do not fear, for now you have another son." [18]With her last breath—for she was at the point of death—she named him Ben-oni; but his father named him Benjamin. [19]Thus Rachel died; and she was buried on the road to Ephrath (now Bethlehem). [20]Jacob set up a sacred pillar on her grave, and the same pillar marks Rachel's grave to this day.

[21]Israel moved on and pitched his tent beyond Migdal-eder. [22]While Israel was encamped in that region, Reuben went and lay with Bilhah, his father's concubine. When Israel heard of it, he was greatly offended.

continue

the monument Jacob set up still marks the spot. Today the site designated as Rachel's tomb remains a place of pilgrimage, especially for pregnant women.

That incident is followed by the very brief note that Reuben, Leah's first son, sleeps with Bilhah, Rachel's maid, and Jacob finds out about it. Other biblical stories point to taking the concubine of the conquered enemy as a symbol of taking the defeated kingdom (see 2 Sam 3:7-8; 12:7-8; and 1 Kgs 2:13-25). In this case there is no further comment about the incident until Jacob condemns the act in his final testament in 49:3-4. Reuben's act backfires; he loses the birthright to which he is entitled as Jacob's first son just as Jacob's older brother Esau had done. A brief genealogical note follows in verses 22b-26, listing Jacob's twelve sons according to their mothers. Dinah is not included in the list.

The sons of Jacob were now twelve. ²³The sons of Leah: Reuben, Jacob's firstborn, Simeon, Levi, Judah, Issachar, and Zebulun; ²⁴ the sons of Rachel: Joseph and Benjamin; ²⁵the sons of Rachel's maidservant Bilhah: Dan and Naphtali; ²⁶the sons of Leah's maidservant Zilpah: Gad and Asher. These are the sons of Jacob who were born to him in Paddan-aram.

²⁷Jacob went home to his father Isaac at Mamre, in Kiriath-arba (now Hebron), where Abraham and Isaac had resided. ²⁸The length of Isaac's life was one hundred and eighty years; ²⁹then he breathed his last. He died as an old man and was gathered to his people. After a full life, his sons Esau and Jacob buried him.

CHAPTER 36

Edomite Lists

¹These are the descendants of Esau (that is, Edom). ² Esau took his wives from among the Canaanite women: Adah, daughter of Elon the Hittite; Oholibamah, the daughter of Anah the son of Zibeon the Hivite; ³and Basemath, daughter of Ishmael and sister of Nebaioth. ⁴Adah bore Eliphaz to Esau; Basemath bore Reuel; ⁵and Oholibamah bore Jeush, Jalam and Korah. These are the sons of Esau who were born to him in the land of Canaan.

⁶Esau took his wives, his sons, his daughters, and all the members of his household, as well as his livestock, all his cattle, and all the property he had acquired in the land of Canaan, and went to the land of Seir, away from his brother Jacob. ⁷Their possessions had become too great for them to dwell together, and the land in which they were residing could not support them because of their livestock. ⁸So Esau settled in the highlands of Seir. (Esau is Edom.) ⁹These are the descendants of Esau, ancestor of the Edomites, in the highlands of Seir.

¹⁰These are the names of the sons of Esau: Eliphaz, son of Adah, wife of Esau, and Reuel, son of Basemath, wife of Esau. ¹¹ The sons of Eliphaz were Teman, Omar, Zepho, Gatam, and Kenaz. ¹²Timna was a concubine of Eliphaz, the son of Esau, and she bore Amalek to Eliphaz. Those were the sons of Adah, the wife of Esau. ¹³These were the sons of Reuel: Nahath, Zerah, Shammah, and Mizzah. Those were the sons of Basemath, the wife of Esau. ¹⁴These were the sons of Esau's wife Oholibamah—the daughter of Anah, son of Zibeon—whom she bore to Esau: Jeush, Jalam, and Korah.

¹⁵These are the clans of the sons of Esau. The sons of Eliphaz, Esau's firstborn: the clans of Teman, Omar, Zepho, Kenaz, ¹⁶Korah, Gatam, and Amalek. These are the clans of Eliphaz in the land of Edom; they are the sons of Adah. ¹⁷These are the sons of Reuel, son of Esau: the clans of Nahath, Zerah, Shammah, and Mizzah. These are the clans of Reuel in the land of Edom; they are the sons of Basemath, wife of Esau. ¹⁸These were the sons of Oholibamah, wife of Esau: the clans of Jeush, Jalam, and Korah. These are the clans of Esau's wife Oholibamah, daughter of Anah. ¹⁹These are the sons of Esau—that is, Edom—according to their clans.

²⁰These are the sons of Seir the Horite, the inhabitants of the land: Lotan, Shobal, Zibeon, Anah, ²¹Dishon, Ezer, and Dishan; those are the clans of the Horites, sons of Seir in the land of Edom. ²² The sons of Lotan were Hori and Hemam, and Lotan's sister was Timna. ²³These are the sons of Shobal: Alvan, Mahanath, Ebal, Shepho, and Onam. ²⁴These are the sons of Zibeon: Aiah and Anah. He is the Anah who found water in the desert while he was pasturing the donkeys of his father Zibeon. ²⁵These are the children of Anah: Dishon and Oholibamah, daughter of Anah. ²⁶These are the sons of Dishon: Hemdan, Eshban, Ithran, and Cheran. ²⁷These are the sons of Ezer: Bilhan, Zaavan, and Akan. ²⁸These are the sons of Dishan: Uz and Aran. ²⁹These are the clans of the Horites: the clans of Lotan, Shobal, Zibeon, Anah, ³⁰Dishon, Ezer, and Dishan; those are the clans of the Horites, clan by clan, in the land of Seir.

³¹These are the kings who reigned in the land of Edom before any king reigned over the Israelites. ³²Bela, son of Beor, became king in Edom; the name of his city was Dinhabah. ³³When Bela

continue

A second brief note observes that Jacob returns to his father Isaac at Mamre, the place where both Isaac and Abraham had lived. Then Isaac dies and his two sons bury him, just as Isaac and Ishmael buried their father Abraham. In both instances, despite all the tensions among the siblings, they honor their fathers in death. Isaac's role in life was to carry forward the divine promises; he lives to see them handed over to his son Jacob.

36:1-43 Esau's descendants

A detailed genealogy of Esau's descendants follows, interspersed with two other lists, the indigenous tribes of Seir and the Edomite kings. The lists are complicated because some of the information is given elsewhere, with a few variations. Verses 1-8 give the names of Esau's three wives and their children and grandchildren. Here the wives' names are Adah, a Hittite; Oholibamah, a Hivite; and Basemath, daughter of Ishmael; these differ slightly from the names given in 26:34 and 28:9: Judith, Basemath, and Mahalath. Adah and Basemath (according to the list in chapter 36) both bear one son to Esau; Oholibamah bears three.

Verses 9-14 list the children born to each of Esau's wives in Seir, where they settle after Jacob returns home. Adah's son has six sons of whom one is born to a concubine, and Basemath's son has four sons. The list does not name the grandsons of Basemath. The names

died, Jobab, son of Zerah, from Bozrah, succeeded him as king. [34]When Jobab died, Husham, from the land of the Temanites, succeeded him as king. [35]When Husham died, Hadad, son of Bedad, succeeded him as king. He is the one who defeated Midian in the country of Moab; the name of his city was Avith. [36]When Hadad died, Samlah, from Masrekah, succeeded him as king. [37]When Samlah died, Shaul, from Rehoboth-on-the-River, succeeded him as king. [38]When Shaul died, Baal-hanan, son of Achbor, succeeded him as king. [39]When Baal-hanan, son of Achbor, died, Hadad succeeded him as king; the name of his city was Pau. His wife's name was Mehetabel, the daughter of Matred, son of Mezahab.

continue

are repeated in verses 15-19 with the inclusion of one additional grandson to Adah's descendants. Amalek, the son of the concubine, is listed as a full son with his brothers.

Verses 20-30 list the descendants of Seir, who become seven clans. Then verses 31-39 name the eight kings of Edom who ruled before the establishment of the monarchy in Israel. Finally, verses 40-43 name the eleven Edomite clans. These lists, attributed to P, represent the fulfillment of Isaac's blessing to Esau in 27:39-40: Esau will live far away and will be a warrior rather than a farmer. They also fulfill the Lord's words to Rebekah when the twins were still in her womb (25:23) that the older would serve the younger: Esau's descendants eventually serve the descendants of Jacob.

The lists attest to the long history of the early inhabitants of the land, and illustrate the ongoing intermingling of the peoples throughout history. They also witness to the ongoing divine protection of the people throughout all their comings and goings in the region. After these genealogical notes the focus of the narrative shifts to Jacob's son Joseph, the first son of his beloved wife Rachel, who died giving birth to her second son Benjamin.

⁴⁰These are the names of the clans of Esau identified according to their families and localities: the clans of Timna, Alvah, Jetheth, ⁴¹Oholibamah, Elah, Pinon, ⁴²Kenaz, Teman, Mibzar, ⁴³Magdiel, and Iram. Those are the clans of the Edomites, according to their settlements in their territorial holdings—that is, of Esau, the ancestor of the Edomites.

CHAPTER 37

Joseph Sold into Egypt

¹Jacob settled in the land where his father had sojourned, the land of Canaan. ²This is the story of the family of Jacob. When Joseph was seventeen years old, he was tending the flocks with his brothers; he was an assistant to the sons of his father's wives Bilhah and Zilpah, and Joseph brought their father bad reports about them. ³Israel loved Joseph best of all his sons, for he was the child of his old age; and he had made him a long ornamented tunic. ⁴When his brothers saw that their father loved him best of all his brothers, they hated him so much that they could not say a kind word to him.

⁵Once Joseph had a dream, and when he told his brothers, they hated him even more. ⁶He said to them, "Listen to this dream I had. ⁷There we were, binding sheaves in the field, when suddenly my sheaf rose to an upright position, and your sheaves formed a ring around my sheaf and bowed down to it." ⁸His brothers said to him, "Are you really going to make yourself king over us? Will you rule over us?" So they hated him all the more because of his dreams and his reports.

⁹Then he had another dream, and told it to his brothers. "Look, I had another dream," he said; "this time, the sun and the moon and eleven stars were bowing down to me." ¹⁰When he told it to his father and his brothers, his father reproved him and asked, "What is the meaning of this dream of yours? Can it be that I and your mother and your brothers are to come and bow to the ground before you?" ¹¹So his brothers were furious at him but his father kept the matter in mind.

continue

THE ANCESTRAL STORY
PART 4: THE JOSEPH STORY

Genesis 37:1–50:26

Both the focus and the genre of the narrative shift at this point. While the ancestral story in chapters 12–36 consists of a series of anecdotes arranged in episodic order (that is, separate episodes, loosely connected to one another but not moving toward a climax), the Joseph story has a unified plot that reaches toward a climax. The narrative is called a novella, or short novel. The term implies that the story is fictional; in fact, just as we do not know the precise historicity of the previous chapters, neither do we know the exact historical details of the Joseph narrative. What we do know is that the ancient narrative recounts God's continuing care for the people as promised from the time of Noah to the people in general, and promised in particular to Abraham and his family. The story of Joseph relates that ongoing care for the people as they move to Egypt, setting the stage for the exodus to come.

We have seen that the sons of Leah have a penchant for getting into trouble. Here we learn that the sons of Jacob's beloved, deceased Rachel, and especially Joseph her firstborn, are their father's favorites. This favoritism exacerbates the relationships among the twelve brothers, creating the conditions for several complications, expressed in familiar themes that continue to weave their way through the narrative; for example, competition among the brothers, similar to that between wives and brothers in previous generations; and younger versus older as was the case between Esau and Jacob, and between Ishmael and Isaac.

Articles of clothing figure prominently here. Likewise, dreams also play a prominent part in the story, as does the theme of divine promise in jeopardy, protected by God. The story also records reversals of various kinds: in geographic locations, weather conditions, relationships among the family members, the fortunes of different brothers, Jacob's hopes and fears, to name a few. A further characteristic of the story is the influence of the wisdom tradition, which emphasizes human wit. Divine intervention is indirect: there are no visions, but the narrative specifies at different points that God continues to direct the affairs of Joseph and his family.

37:1-36 The sale of Joseph into slavery

The story resumes where it left off at the end of chapter 35: Jacob and his family are settled in Hebron. The narrative now focuses on Joseph, a seventeen-year-old shepherd who works with his brothers. The narrative immediately introduces the tension among the brothers, reporting that Joseph tells his father tales on Bilhah's and Zilpah's sons, with whom he works as an assistant (he is younger than ten of his brothers and also his sister Dinah). We are not told whether his reports to his father are true or false, only that Joseph breaks ranks with his brothers by reporting on them. Then the cause of the tension is revealed: Joseph is his father's favorite, and his father singles him out for preferential treatment.

Jacob gives Joseph a special garment. This item has been the subject of much discussion and illustration, including the title of the musical *Joseph and the Amazing Technicolor Dreamcoat*. The actual meaning of the Hebrew word is uncertain: translations include a long-sleeved garment, one with many colors or special ornamentation, and one that reaches to the floor. While the meaning is uncertain, the idea is clear: Joseph receives a special garment from his father who dotes on him, and this creates bitter envy and rivalry on the part of his brothers, to the point that they can barely speak to him.

Joseph has a talent for interpreting dreams, understood in the ancient world as a gift from God, since dreams were thought to be divine revelations. In the Joseph narrative the dreams are symbolic in contrast to the straightforward words from God in earlier chapters of Genesis. The dreams appear in pairs, with different symbols giving the same message. This duplication assures that the dreams are genuine, and that their message is clear.

Joseph's report of his dreams exacerbates the tension between his brothers and him for

¹²One day, when his brothers had gone to pasture their father's flocks at Shechem, ¹³Israel said to Joseph, "Are your brothers not tending our flocks at Shechem? Come and I will send you to them." "I am ready," Joseph answered. ¹⁴"Go then," he replied; "see if all is well with your brothers and the flocks, and bring back word." So he sent him off from the valley of Hebron. When Joseph reached Shechem, ¹⁵a man came upon him as he was wandering about in the fields. "What are you looking for?" the man asked him. ¹⁶"I am looking for my brothers," he answered. "Please tell me where they are tending the flocks." ¹⁷The man told him, "They have moved on from here; in fact, I heard them say, 'Let us go on to Dothan.'" So Joseph went after his brothers and found them in Dothan. ¹⁸They saw him from a distance, and before he reached them, they plotted to kill him. ¹⁹They said to one another: "Here comes that dreamer! ²⁰Come now, let us kill him and throw him into one of the cisterns here; we could say that a wild beast devoured him. We will see then what comes of his dreams."

²¹But when Reuben heard this, he tried to save him from their hands, saying: "We must not take his life." ²²Then Reuben said, "Do not shed blood! Throw him into this cistern in the wilderness; but do not lay a hand on him." His purpose was to save him from their hands and restore him to his father.

²³So when Joseph came up to his brothers, they stripped him of his tunic, the long ornamented tunic he had on; ²⁴then they took him and threw him into the cistern. The cistern was empty; there was no water in it.

²⁵Then they sat down to eat. Looking up, they saw a caravan of Ishmaelites coming from Gilead, their camels laden with gum, balm, and resin to be taken down to Egypt. ²⁶Judah said to his brothers: "What is to be gained by killing our brother and concealing his blood? ²⁷Come, let us sell him to these Ishmaelites, instead of doing away with him ourselves. After all, he is our brother, our own flesh." His brothers agreed. ²⁸Midianite traders

continue

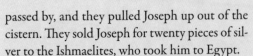

passed by, and they pulled Joseph up out of the cistern. They sold Joseph for twenty pieces of silver to the Ishmaelites, who took him to Egypt.

²⁹When Reuben went back to the cistern and saw that Joseph was not in it, he tore his garments, ³⁰and returning to his brothers, he exclaimed: "The boy is gone! And I—where can I turn?" ³¹They took Joseph's tunic, and after slaughtering a goat, dipped the tunic in its blood. ³²Then they sent someone to bring the long ornamented tunic to their father, with the message: "We found this. See whether it is your son's tunic or not." ³³He recognized it and exclaimed: "My son's tunic! A wild beast has devoured him! Joseph has been torn to pieces!" ³⁴Then Jacob tore his garments, put sackcloth on his loins, and mourned his son many days. ³⁵Though his sons and daughters tried to console him, he refused all consolation, saying, "No, I will go down mourning to my son in Sheol." Thus did his father weep for him.

³⁶The Midianites, meanwhile, sold Joseph in Egypt to Potiphar, an official of Pharaoh and his chief steward.

CHAPTER 38

Judah and Tamar

¹About that time Judah went down, away from his brothers, and pitched his tent near a certain Adullamite named Hirah. ²There Judah saw the daughter of a Canaanite named Shua; he married her, and had intercourse with her. ³She conceived and bore a son, whom she named Er. ⁴Again she conceived and bore a son, whom she named Onan. ⁵Then she bore still another son, whom she named Shelah. She was in Chezib when she bore him.

⁶Judah got a wife named Tamar for his first-born, Er. ⁷But Er, Judah's firstborn, greatly offended the LORD; so the LORD took his life. ⁸Then Judah said to Onan, "Have intercourse with your brother's wife, in fulfillment of your duty as brother-in-law, and thus preserve your brother's line." ⁹Onan, however, knew that the offspring would not be his; so whenever he had intercourse

continue

two reasons: first, because the fact of his having the dreams singles him out as the recipient of a special gift; and second, because of the subject of the dreams. Both the dream of the crops and that of the stars deliver the same message: his brothers will be subservient to him. Here the younger-older motif begins to factor into the story.

The second dream includes not only his brothers but also his parents among those who will be subservient to him. The mention of his mother is puzzling here since she has already died (35:19). Even Jacob questions Joseph about the second dream, but he "kept the matter in mind" (37:11). Throughout his own life Jacob received significant revelations in dreams; he can appreciate the importance of his son's dreams.

In Jacob's case it was his mother Rebekah who arranged that Jacob would receive his father's blessing, thus depriving Esau of what was rightfully his and feeding the tension between the two brothers. Now Jacob himself feeds the tension between Joseph and his brothers by showing favoritism to him. Joseph's awkwardly privileged position comes, then, partly from his father's actions and partly from the dreams.

In verse 13 Jacob sends Joseph to his brothers, who are tending the flocks at Shechem. Joseph's response, "hinneni," recalls other willing responses on the part of the ancestors when they are asked to do some significant task. Here Jacob directs Joseph to find his brothers and bring back a report on them. Perhaps he is concerned about their safety after their disastrous destruction of Shechem in chapter 34. The brothers have continued to move along with the grazing flocks, so by the time Joseph finds them they are at a considerable distance from home. The distance gives the brothers the opportunity to devise a plot against him without likelihood of detection: they plan to kill him and throw him into a cistern. Such an end would deprive Joseph of a proper burial, and thus dishonor him and them; the brothers are blinded to this possibility by their hatred and envy of him.

Reuben, the firstborn son, objects to killing his brother and offers an alternative: that they simply throw him into the cistern and not kill him. The narrative adds that Reuben hopes to rescue Joseph and return him to Jacob. As first-born, he made an unsuccessful bid for power in violating Bilhah (35:22); here he unsuccessfully attempts to use his position in a positive way. Joseph reaches his brothers, wearing the infamous garment, which his brothers take from him; they throw him into the empty cistern, then sit down to enjoy a meal, indifferent to Joseph's plight and to their own evil.

In verse 25 the unexpected arrival of Ishmaelites offers an alternative opportunity, and the brothers arrange to sell their brother. (Egypt had a slave trade at the time.) Ironically, they explain their own hesitation to kill him because he is their brother, but that does not stop them from selling him or from deceiving their father about what they have done to him. A further irony rests in the family relationship among the descendants of Abraham: the brothers sell Joseph to their own relatives. (Recall that Ishmael was the son of Abraham by Hagar, the Egyptian maidservant of Sarah.) The mention of Midianites in verse 28 is puzzling. It might be a detail from the E strand in a passage that is primarily a J and P story, or it might relate that Joseph is sold several times before the Ishmaelites purchase him. Twenty shekels is the price of a slave between the ages of five and twenty, according to both the Code of Hammurabi and Leviticus 27:5; the weight of the pieces of silver in this passage is not known, but is most likely comparable. The passage very likely predates Leviticus, with the detail about the price coming from a later P insertion.

Reuben is not with his brothers when they sell Joseph. Later, when Reuben returns to the cistern to retrieve him, he discovers that Joseph is gone. The text is ambiguous as to whether his brothers know about his plan to rescue Joseph. But his anguished question expresses his consternation when he realizes Joseph is gone.

In verse 31 the brothers determine a way to break the news of Joseph's disappearance to their father. They use the infamous garment and the blood of a kid, two items that Jacob used long ago when he deceived his own father into giving him the blessing intended for Esau. When Jacob receives the bloody garment, his three exclamations show his gradual realization of what it means: his beloved son Joseph is dead (37:33). Joseph's robe is the sign of his apparent death; Jacob's torn clothes are the sign of his grief. (Tearing one's garment was the customary sign of mourning.) Sheol, where Jacob expects to go after death, was the place deep under the earth where the spirits of all the deceased were believed to rest forever. It was not a place of reward or punishment.

Here the reader knows that Joseph is still alive. Jacob assumes his son is dead, and it is not clear what Joseph's brothers know about him. Meanwhile, the Midianites sell him into slavery to Potiphar, a courtier in the court of Pharaoh. This development jeopardizes the longstanding promise of descendants to Abraham, Isaac, and Jacob: Joseph is clearly his father's favorite and the one on whom we assume the promise rests; now he is a slave in Egypt.

38:1-30 Judah and Tamar

On the surface chapter 38 appears to be a digression from the Joseph narrative, but a closer look shows its connection. The narrative is vague about the chronology, stating simply, "About that time." Judah, who encouraged his brothers to sell Joseph rather than kill him, leaves his brothers and settles near Hirah the Adullamite. He marries a Canaanite woman and they have three sons. There is no stigma attached to marrying a Canaanite woman, unlike the situations for Isaac and Jacob (24:3; 28:6). Judah makes the customary arrangements for the marriage of his firstborn son Er to Tamar. Er sins (we are not told what his sin was) and the Lord takes his life in punishment. In keeping with the custom, Judah instructs his second son Onan to marry Tamar. Onan refuses to cooperate, interrupting intercourse and thus avoiding the conception of a child with Tamar. It is not clear whether he refuses to honor his deceased brother's name or whether he does not want to share his inheritance with a son. Whatever the reason, his negligence with regard to Tamar is a sin of with his brother's wife, he wasted his seed on the ground, to avoid giving offspring to his brother. ¹⁰What he did greatly offended the LORD, and the LORD took his life too. ¹¹Then Judah said to his daughter-in-law Tamar, "Remain a widow in your father's house until my son Shelah grows up"—for he feared that Shelah also might die like his brothers. So Tamar went to live in her father's house.

¹²Time passed, and the daughter of Shua, Judah's wife, died. After Judah completed the period of mourning, he went up to Timnah, to those who were shearing his sheep, in company with his friend Hirah the Adullamite. ¹³Then Tamar was told, "Your father-in-law is on his way up to Timnah to shear his sheep." ¹⁴So she took off her widow's garments, covered herself with a shawl, and having wrapped herself sat down at the entrance to Enaim, which is on the way to Timnah; for she was aware that, although Shelah was now grown up, she had not been given to him in marriage. ¹⁵When Judah saw her, he thought she was a harlot, since she had covered her face. ¹⁶So he went over to her at the roadside and said, "Come, let me have intercourse with you," for he did not realize that she was his daughter-in-law. She replied, "What will you pay me for letting you have intercourse with me?" ¹⁷He answered, "I will send you a young goat from the flock." "Very well," she said, "provided you leave me a pledge until you send it." ¹⁸Judah asked, "What pledge should I leave you?" She answered, "Your seal and cord, and the staff in your hand." So he gave them to her and had intercourse with her, and she conceived by him. ¹⁹After she got up and went away, she took off her shawl and put on her widow's garments again.

²⁰Judah sent the young goat by his friend the Adullamite to recover the pledge from the woman; but he did not find her. ²¹So he asked the men of that place, "Where is the prostitute, the one by the roadside in Enaim?" But they answered, "No prostitute has been here." ²²He went back to Judah and told him, "I did not find her; and besides, the men of the place said, 'No prostitute has been here.'" ²³"Let her keep the things,"

continue

disobedience for which the Lord takes Onan's life, leaving Judah with only one living son. At the time the levirate duty of a father-in-law to give his next son to the widow was obligatory; later law provided for the son to refuse this duty (Deut 25:5-9).

Judah does not wish to lose his only living son (v. 11) , so he puts Tamar in an impossible position: he sends her back to her father's house, but does not release her from his family. Consequently she does not really belong to her father's family, but neither is she under the protection of Judah.

Years later Tamar takes an opportunity to force Judah's responsibility toward her (v. 12). She dresses like a prostitute (again clothing factors into the story) and places herself where he will see her as he travels to shear his sheep. The text is careful not to judge him harshly: he does not recognize her because of her veil, and he had not planned to engage a prostitute, as he has nothing with which to pay her. (The usual fee was a kid.) Instead, she requests three items that can positively identify him: his seal, cord, and staff. Cylinder seals with a hole through the middle, through which a cord was run to hang the seals around the neck of their owners, were a means of marking documents: the seal was rolled in soft clay. When the clay hardened the mark of the seal remained, identifying the sender of the document and assuring that it had not been tampered with. The staff or walking stick probably had some particular mark of identification on it.

Tamar conceives a child, and returns to her widow's life. Judah, true to his word, sends his friend Hirah to deliver the promised goat to Tamar (v. 20). Just as a kid played a role in notifying Jacob that Joseph was thought to be dead, likewise a kid plays a role here in maintaining Judah's anonymity. Hirah inquires about the whereabouts of a cult prostitute, but there is no cult prostitute in the town. (Tamar posed as a prostitute, not a cult prostitute. The Hebrew words mark this distinction.) Hirah reports to Judah that he is unable to locate the woman, and Judah prefers to let the matter go rather than risk embarrassment.

In verse 24 Judah learns that Tamar is pregnant, but has no idea that he is the child's father. Acting on his authority as head of the family, he orders that she be burned, an exceptionally harsh means of death. But Tamar produces the three items to identify the father of her child, and Judah realizes what he has done. Tamar's words to Judah resemble those of the messenger who delivers Joseph's garment to Jacob in 37:32. Judah acknowledges his sin: he did not give his third son to Tamar, as the ancient custom required. He uses his prerogative as her father-in-law to condemn her, but he neglected to use it earlier when he refused to give his third son to her. Again the text is careful not to condemn him harshly: it specifies that he does not have intercourse with her again. The narrative also exonerates Tamar: Judah says about her, "She is in the right rather than I" (38:26). In fact, Judah placed Tamar in an impossible position by not giving his third son Shelah to her but at the same time not relieving her of any obligation to him as her father-in-law. Tamar does what is necessary to provide a son for her deceased husband and still remain faithful to her obligations as Judah's daughter-in-law.

Tamar gives birth to twins in verse 27. The red thread tied around the first hand to come out of the womb recalls the birth of Rebekah's twins: Esau, whose name means "red," was born first but was not the favored son (25:25-26). Zerah is Tamar's firstborn, but Perez, the second, is the favored one; we learn in Ruth 4:18-22 that he is the ancestor of David.

The chapter began by depicting Leah's fourth son in trouble, like her first three. But it ends with indications that he assumes responsibility for his actions. The next time we meet Judah is in 43:3, when he and his brothers are back at home with their father.

39:1-23 Joseph in the household of Potiphar

The Joseph story resumes where it left off in 37:36, with Joseph in the household of Potiphar, his new owner. For the first time in the Joseph story we read that the Lord is with

Judah replied; "otherwise we will become a laughingstock. After all, I did send her this young goat, but you did not find her."

²⁴About three months later, Judah was told, "Your daughter-in-law Tamar has acted like a harlot and now she is pregnant from her harlotry." Judah said, "Bring her out; let her be burned." ²⁵But as she was being brought out, she sent word to her father-in-law, "It is by the man to whom these things belong that I am pregnant." Then she said, "See whose seal and cord and staff these are." ²⁶Judah recognized them and said, "She is in the right rather than I, since I did not give her to my son Shelah." He had no further sexual relations with her.

²⁷When the time of her delivery came, there were twins in her womb. ²⁸While she was giving birth, one put out his hand; and the midwife took and tied a crimson thread on his hand, noting, "This one came out first." ²⁹But as he withdrew his hand, his brother came out; and she said, "What a breach you have made for yourself!" So he was called Perez. ³⁰Afterward his brother, who had the crimson thread on his hand, came out; he was called Zerah.

CHAPTER 39

Joseph's Temptation

¹When Joseph was taken down to Egypt, an Egyptian, Potiphar, an official of Pharaoh and his chief steward, bought him from the Ishmaelites who had brought him there. ²The Lord was with Joseph and he enjoyed great success and was assigned to the household of his Egyptian master. ³When his master saw that the Lord was with him and brought him success in whatever he did, ⁴he favored Joseph and made him his personal attendant; he put him in charge of his household and entrusted to him all his possessions. ⁵From the moment that he put him in charge of his household and all his possessions, the Lord blessed the Egyptian's house for Joseph's sake; the Lord's blessing was on everything he owned, both inside the house and out. ⁶Having left everything he owned in Joseph's charge, he gave no

continue

thought, with Joseph there, to anything but the food he ate.

Now Joseph was well-built and handsome. [7]After a time, his master's wife looked at him with longing and said, "Lie with me." [8]But he refused and said to his master's wife, "Look, as long as I am here, my master does not give a thought to anything in the house, but has entrusted to me all he owns. [9]He has no more authority in this house than I do. He has withheld from me nothing but you, since you are his wife. How, then, could I do this great wrong and sin against God?" [10]Although she spoke to him day after day, he would not agree to lie with her, or even be near her.

[11]One such day, when Joseph came into the house to do his work, and none of the household servants were then in the house, [12]she laid hold of him by his cloak, saying, "Lie with me!" But leaving the cloak in her hand, he escaped and ran outside. [13]When she saw that he had left his cloak in her hand as he escaped outside, [14]she cried out to her household servants and told them, "Look! My husband has brought us a Hebrew man to mock us! He came in here to lie with me, but I cried out loudly. [15]When he heard me scream, he left his cloak beside me and escaped and ran outside."

[16]She kept the cloak with her until his master came home. [17]Then she told him the same story: "The Hebrew slave whom you brought us came to me to amuse himself at my expense. [18]But when I screamed, he left his cloak beside me and escaped outside." [19]When the master heard his wife's story in which she reported, "Thus and so your servant did to me," he became enraged. [20]Joseph's master seized him and put him into the jail where the king's prisoners were confined. And there he sat, in jail.

[21]But the LORD was with Joseph, and showed him kindness by making the chief jailer well-disposed toward him. [22]The chief jailer put Joseph in charge of all the prisoners in the jail. Everything that had to be done there, he was the one to do it. [23]The chief jailer did not have to look after any-

continue

Joseph. Throughout the Joseph story the Lord guides and protects Joseph, but the narrative seldom mentions him. In this chapter, however, the word "Lord" appears six times. Its only other appearance in the Joseph story is in Jacob's testament in 49:18. The word "God" appears much more frequently in the Joseph story.

Here another of Jacob's sons faces a critical situation with a woman. (Jacob himself had his own difficulties over women: he was given Leah, after being promised Rachel for a wife in 29:14-30.) Joseph fares well under Potiphar, thanks to divine protection and guidance. Furthermore, he is handsome, an additional sign of divine favor. His master leaves all the household responsibilities to Joseph. The description of Potiphar being attentive only to the food he eats suggests that he neglects his wife. The juxtaposition of contrasting descriptions of Potiphar and Joseph foreshadows trouble in his household, and it is not long in coming.

Potiphar's wife's speaks as a slave owner to a slave in her efforts to seduce him (v. 7). Joseph attributes his refusal to his faithfulness both to Potiphar and to God. But she refuses to give up, and finds a way when the two are alone. Once again Joseph's garment is a source of trouble for him. She takes it to use against him by blackmailing him, just as his brothers did earlier when they took the garment his father gave him, and used it to insinuate that Joseph was dead. Tamar, on the other hand, took Judah's seal, cord, and staff for a different purpose. She held them in pledge until he would pay his debt to her, and eventually used them to identify him as the father of her children, saving her own life in the process.

Potiphar's wife is vengeful in her rejection and embarrassment, and she immediately accuses her husband of neglect in bringing a foreigner into the household. She claims to have screamed as evidence of her innocence; eventually the law required such an act if one was raped in a public place (Deut 22:23-27). Potiphar's lack of involvement continues, and he condemns Joseph, to whom he has entrusted his entire household, without even asking for his side of the story. Joseph is imprisoned in the royal prison, but the Lord is with him. The chief jailer puts Joseph in charge of the prison, just as Potiphar put him in charge of his household, and trusts him implicitly.

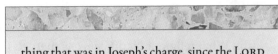

thing that was in Joseph's charge, since the LORD was with him and was bringing success to whatever he was doing.

EXPLORING LESSON THREE

1. a) What religious significance is there to Jacob's instructions preparing his family for the journey to Bethel (35:1-4)?

_____

_____

_____

   b) Why are the promises Jacob receives at Bethel important (35:9-12)? (See 12:1-3; 26:1-5).

_____

_____

_____

2. After Jacob and his family leave Bethel, what are three major events that occur in the life of the family (35:16-22)?

_____

_____

_____

_____

_____

3. In what way is the burial of Isaac (35:27-29) reminiscent of the burial of his father, Abraham (25:7-10)?

_____

_____

_____

_____

4. a) Why is Joseph despised by his older brothers (37:2-4)?

_____

_____

_____

   b) What does Joseph do or say to provoke his brothers' hatred (37:5-11)?

_____

_____

_____

5. How do Reuben and Judah each attempt to intervene in their own way to prevent the murder of Joseph (37:12-28)?

_____

_____

_____

_____

6. Why is Judah responsible for finding Tamar a husband from among his sons (38:1-11)? (See Deut 25:5-10.)

_____

_____

_____

_____

7. How is Joseph's relationship with his older brothers like that of Cain and Abel (4:1-8) and Jacob and Esau (25:19-23; 27:41)?

_____

_____

_____

_____

8. How does Joseph gain favor with Potiphar, then, with his jailer (39:1-23, especially vv. 5 and 23)?

_____

_____

_____

_____

_____

9. Like Joseph, in what ways have you sensed the unseen hand of God helping to guide your life, whether in good times or in bad?

_____

_____

_____

_____

_____

CLOSING PRAYER

Prayer

They saw [Joseph] from a distance, and before he reached them, they plotted to kill him.

(Gen 37:18)

Sometimes, Lord, our rivalries and insecurities get the best of us. We act in ways that harm others, ourselves, and our relationship with you. We acknowledge our sin, the times we have acted either with forethought or impulsively to take revenge, to settle debts, or simply to act without love. We pray for forgiveness and ask for the resolve to repair damages caused or received, especially . . .

LESSON FOUR

Genesis 40–44

Begin your personal study and group discussion with a simple and sincere prayer such as:

Prayer

God of my ancestors in faith, open my eyes and ears and heart as I reflect on these people whom you called centuries ago.

Read the Bible text of Genesis 40–44 found in the outside columns of pages 60–70, highlighting what stands out to you.

Read the accompanying commentary to add to your understanding.

Respond to the questions on pages 71–72, Exploring Lesson Four.

The Closing Prayer on page 73 is for your personal use and may be used at the end of group discussion.

CHAPTER 40

The Dreams Interpreted

¹Some time afterward, the royal cupbearer and baker offended their lord, the king of Egypt. ²Pharaoh was angry with his two officials, the chief cupbearer and the chief baker, ³and he put them in custody in the house of the chief steward, the same jail where Joseph was confined. ⁴The chief steward assigned Joseph to them, and he became their attendant.

After they had been in custody for some time, ⁵the cupbearer and the baker of the king of Egypt who were confined in the jail both had dreams on the same night, each his own dream and each dream with its own meaning. ⁶When Joseph came to them in the morning, he saw that they looked disturbed. ⁷So he asked Pharaoh's officials who were with him in custody in his master's house, "Why do you look so troubled today?" ⁸They answered him, "We have had dreams, but there is no one to interpret them." Joseph said to them, "Do interpretations not come from God? Please tell me the dreams."

⁹Then the chief cupbearer told Joseph his dream. "In my dream," he said, "I saw a vine in front of me, ¹⁰and on the vine were three branches. It had barely budded when its blossoms came out, and its clusters ripened into grapes. ¹¹Pharaoh's cup was in my hand; so I took the grapes, pressed them out into his cup, and put it in Pharaoh's hand." ¹²Joseph said to him: "This is its interpretation. The three branches are three days; ¹³within three days Pharaoh will single you out and restore you to your post. You will be handing Pharaoh his cup as you formerly did when you were his cupbearer. ¹⁴Only think of me when all is well with you, and please do me the great favor of mentioning me to Pharaoh, to get me out of this place. ¹⁵The truth is that I was kidnapped from the land of the Hebrews, and I have not done anything here that they should have put me into a dungeon."

¹⁶When the chief baker saw that Joseph had given a favorable interpretation, he said to him:

continue

40:1-23 Joseph in prison

Eventually Pharaoh has two royal officials incarcerated in the same prison as Joseph. His gift for interpreting dreams serves him well when both officials have troubling dreams in the same night. Joseph offers to interpret the dreams, acknowledging that his ability comes from God. This statement dissociates his ability from that of the magicians in Pharaoh's court, whose duties include interpreting dreams. Both dreams involve the number three, a number that signifies completion. Here the number represents the number of days until the dreams come to pass. Numerology was often associated with wisdom in the ancient world. Joseph's ability to interpret numbers demonstrates that he has the divine gift of wisdom.

The cupbearer's dream, which he repeats in verses 9-11, relates to his duty in the court: as cupbearer he holds the cup from which the Pharaoh drinks. His character must be above reproach because it is his responsibility to be sure no one poisons the Pharaoh. Joseph interprets the dream, announcing to the cupbearer that he will soon be released from prison. Joseph asks in return that the cupbearer arrange for his release as soon as it is possible.

Then the baker repeats his own dream that, like the cupbearer's, relates to his office. This time Joseph's interpretation foreshadows an unfortunate outcome. In three days, the time designated in both dreams, both of Joseph's interpretations prove to be accurate: the cupbearer is restored to his office and the baker is impaled during a birthday banquet in Pharaoh's honor. The cupbearer does not remember Joseph, but completely forgets about him. His forgetting foreshadows the eventual experience of Jacob's descendants in Egypt when "a new king, who knew nothing of Joseph, rose to power" (Exod 1:8).

 The ability to **interpret dreams** is a sign of wisdom. Examples of these gifted wise ones are Joseph (Gen 40:1–41:36); Daniel (Dan 2:14-45; 4:1-24); the magi (Matt 2:12); and Joseph, husband of Mary (Matt 1:20-25; 2:13-15). It is acknowledged that God is the source of the gift (see Dan 2:20-23, 28).

41:1-57 The exoneration of Joseph

Joseph's gift of interpreting dreams continues to serve him well. This time it is Pharaoh who has a troubling dream. It includes several ominous elements: the Nile, on which all the people depend for subsistence, and also cows that figure prominently in the economy of the people. It involves the number seven, a number that denotes completion. Furthermore, it shows the seven unhealthy cows eating the healthy ones. Then, as with Joseph's earlier dream, a second one follows, verifying the message of the first. This one also involves a subsistence item, corn, the number seven, and the unhealthy consuming the healthy. Pharaoh calls on his magicians to interpret the dream. When they fail to do so, the cupbearer finally remembers Joseph.

Verse 14 expresses the urgency of the situation in the rapid succession of preparatory actions. When Pharaoh explains his need to Joseph, Joseph is quick to point out that it is God, not himself, who interprets dreams. He repeats this three more times in his conversation with Pharaoh. Pharaoh reports the dreams

"I too had a dream. In it I had three bread baskets on my head; [17]in the top one were all kinds of bakery products for Pharaoh, but the birds were eating them out of the basket on my head." [18]Joseph said to him in reply: "This is its interpretation. The three baskets are three days; [19]within three days Pharaoh will single you out and will impale you on a stake, and the birds will be eating your flesh."

[20]And so on the third day, which was Pharaoh's birthday, when he gave a banquet to all his servants, he singled out the chief cupbearer and chief baker in the midst of his servants. [21]He restored the chief cupbearer to his office, so that he again handed the cup to Pharaoh; [22]but the chief baker he impaled—just as Joseph had told them in his interpretation. [23]Yet the chief cupbearer did not think of Joseph; he forgot him.

CHAPTER 41

Pharaoh's Dream

[1]After a lapse of two years, Pharaoh had a dream. He was standing by the Nile, [2]when up out of the Nile came seven cows, fine-looking and fat; they grazed in the reed grass. [3]Behind them seven other cows, poor-looking and gaunt, came up out of the Nile; and standing on the bank of the Nile beside the others, [4]the poor-looking, gaunt cows devoured the seven fine-looking, fat cows. Then Pharaoh woke up.

[5]He fell asleep again and had another dream. He saw seven ears of grain, fat and healthy, growing on a single stalk. [6]Behind them sprouted seven ears of grain, thin and scorched by the east wind; [7]and the thin ears swallowed up the seven fat, healthy ears. Then Pharaoh woke up—it was a dream!

[8]Next morning his mind was agitated. So Pharaoh had all the magicians and sages of Egypt summoned and recounted his dream to them; but there was no one to interpret it for him. [9]Then the chief cupbearer said to Pharaoh: "Now I remember my negligence! [10]Once, when Pharaoh

continue

was angry with his servants, he put me and the chief baker in custody in the house of the chief steward. [11]Later, we both had dreams on the same night, and each of our dreams had its own meaning. [12]There was a Hebrew youth with us, a slave of the chief steward; and when we told him our dreams, he interpreted them for us and explained for each of us the meaning of his dream. [13]Things turned out just as he had told us: I was restored to my post, but the other man was impaled."

[14]Pharaoh therefore had Joseph summoned, and they hurriedly brought him from the dungeon. After he shaved and changed his clothes, he came to Pharaoh. [15]Pharaoh then said to Joseph: "I had a dream but there was no one to interpret it. But I hear it said of you, 'If he hears a dream he can interpret it.'" [16]"It is not I," Joseph replied to Pharaoh, "but God who will respond for the well-being of Pharaoh."

[17]Then Pharaoh said to Joseph: "In my dream, I was standing on the bank of the Nile, [18]when up from the Nile came seven cows, fat and well-formed; they grazed in the reed grass. [19]Behind them came seven other cows, scrawny, most ill-formed and gaunt. Never have I seen such bad specimens as these in all the land of Egypt! [20]The gaunt, bad cows devoured the first seven fat cows. [21]But when they had consumed them, no one could tell that they had done so, because they looked as bad as before. Then I woke up. [22]In another dream I saw seven ears of grain, full and healthy, growing on a single stalk. [23]Behind them sprouted seven ears of grain, shriveled and thin and scorched by the east wind; [24]and the seven thin ears swallowed up the seven healthy ears. I have spoken to the magicians, but there is no one to explain it to me."

[25]Joseph said to Pharaoh: "Pharaoh's dreams have the same meaning. God has made known to Pharaoh what he is about to do. [26]The seven healthy cows are seven years, and the seven healthy ears are seven years—the same in each dream. [27]The seven thin, bad cows that came up after them are seven years, as are the seven thin ears scorched

by the east wind; they are seven years of famine. [28]Things are just as I told Pharaoh: God has revealed to Pharaoh what he is about to do. [29]Seven years of great abundance are now coming throughout the land of Egypt; [30]but seven years of famine will rise up after them, when all the abundance will be forgotten in the land of Egypt. When the famine has exhausted the land, [31]no trace of the abundance will be found in the land because of the famine that follows it, for it will be very severe. [32]That Pharaoh had the same dream twice means that the matter has been confirmed by God and that God will soon bring it about.

[33]"Therefore, let Pharaoh seek out a discerning and wise man and put him in charge of the land of Egypt. [34]Let Pharaoh act and appoint overseers for the land to organize it during the seven years of abundance. [35]They should collect all the food of these coming good years, gathering the grain under Pharaoh's authority, for food in the cities, and they should guard it. [36]This food will serve as a reserve for the country against the seven years of famine that will occur in the land of Egypt, so that the land may not perish in the famine."

[37]This advice pleased Pharaoh and all his servants. [38]"Could we find another like him," Pharaoh asked his servants, "a man so endowed with the spirit of God?" [39]So Pharaoh said to Joseph: "Since God has made all this known to you, there is no one as discerning and wise as you are. [40]You shall be in charge of my household, and all my people will obey your command. Only in respect to the throne will I outrank you." [41]Then Pharaoh said to Joseph, "Look, I put you in charge of the whole land of Egypt." [42]With that, Pharaoh took off his signet ring and put it on Joseph's finger. He dressed him in robes of fine linen and put a gold chain around his neck. [43]He then had him ride in his second chariot, and they shouted "Abrek!" before him.

Thus was Joseph installed over the whole land of Egypt. [44]"I am Pharaoh," he told Joseph, "but without your approval no one shall lift hand or foot in all the land of Egypt." [45]Pharaoh also bestowed the name of Zaphenath-paneah on Joseph,

continue

to Joseph, adding details that highlight his anxiety. For instance, he says about the cows, "Never have I seen such bad specimens as these in all the land of Egypt!" (41:19).

Joseph immediately explains to Pharaoh that the dreams are a revelation from God about what the next fourteen years will bring: seven years of plenty, followed by seven years of severe famine. Joseph offers a plan to prepare for the coming famine by stockpiling the surplus during the seven years of plenty to tide the people over during the impending years of famine. Pharaoh is so impressed with Joseph's wise advice that he makes him second in command only to himself, hoping that God will care for Egypt through Joseph (vv. 37-41). There is an implicit statement of faith in God here: Pharaoh relies on the God of Israel rather than on the Egyptian deities to see them through the imminent crisis.

An installation ceremony follows, beginning in verse 42. Once again clothes factor into the story when Pharaoh clothes Joseph in the trappings of rank: signet ring, linen robes, and chain around his neck. The three items are a flashback to the Tamar story: seal, cord, and staff were Judah's identification; here seal, chain, and linen robe are Pharaoh's signs of office. Then he is given a public ride in a royal chariot, probably horse-drawn. This is the first mention of the vehicle in the Bible. The meaning of the salute, "Abrek!" is not known; it is similar to an Egyptian word that means "Attention!" Joseph's new name is Egyptian, and has been interpreted several ways that relate to his gift for interpreting dreams or his new position in Pharaoh's court. His marriage makes him a member of a noble family (41:45). Joseph implements his plan of storing food during the time of plenty so it will be available for the time of famine. The surplus is huge beyond measure.

During the time of prosperity Joseph fathers two sons, Manasseh and Ephraim (vv. 50-52), whose names relate to Joseph's past difficulties and present circumstances. Then the famine comes as predicted, and Pharaoh relies on Joseph to distribute the surplus grain so that ev-

and he gave him in marriage Asenath, the daughter of Potiphera, priest of Heliopolis. And Joseph went out over the land of Egypt. [46]Joseph was thirty years old when he entered the service of Pharaoh, king of Egypt.

After Joseph left Pharaoh, he went throughout the land of Egypt. [47]During the seven years of plenty, when the land produced abundant crops, [48]he collected all the food of these years of plenty that the land of Egypt was enjoying and stored it in the cities, placing in each city the crops of the fields around it. [49]Joseph collected grain like the sands of the sea, so much that at last he stopped measuring it, for it was beyond measure.

[50]Before the famine years set in, Joseph became the father of two sons, borne to him by Asenath, daughter of Potiphera, priest of Heliopolis. [51]Joseph named his firstborn Manasseh, meaning, "God has made me forget entirely my troubles and my father's house"; [52]and the second he named Ephraim, meaning, "God has made me fruitful in the land of my affliction."

[53]When the seven years of abundance enjoyed by the land of Egypt came to an end, [54]the seven years of famine set in, just as Joseph had said. Although there was famine in all the other countries, food was available throughout the land of Egypt. [55]When all the land of Egypt became hungry and the people cried to Pharaoh for food, Pharaoh said to all the Egyptians: "Go to Joseph and do whatever he tells you." [56]When the famine had spread throughout the land, Joseph opened all the cities that had grain and rationed it to the Egyptians, since the famine had gripped the land of Egypt. [57]Indeed, the whole world came to Egypt to Joseph to buy grain, for famine had gripped the whole world.

continue

eryone has plenty to eat. Eventually people come to Egypt from all over the world, seeking relief from the famine. This development sets the stage for Joseph's brothers to come to Egypt and be reunited with their brother.

CHAPTER 42

The Brothers' First Journey to Egypt

¹When Jacob learned that grain rations were for sale in Egypt, he said to his sons: "Why do you keep looking at one another?" ²He went on, "I hear that grain is for sale in Egypt. Go down there and buy some for us, that we may stay alive and not die." ³So ten of Joseph's brothers went down to buy grain from Egypt. ⁴But Jacob did not send Joseph's brother Benjamin with his brothers, for he thought some disaster might befall him. ⁵And so the sons of Israel were among those who came to buy grain, since there was famine in the land of Canaan.

⁶Joseph, as governor of the country, was the one who sold grain to all the people of the land. When Joseph's brothers came, they bowed down to him with their faces to the ground. ⁷He recognized them as soon as he saw them. But he concealed his own identity from them and spoke harshly to them. "Where do you come from?" he asked them. They answered, "From the land of Canaan, to buy food."

⁸When Joseph recognized his brothers, although they did not recognize him, ⁹he was reminded of the dreams he had about them. He said to them: "You are spies. You have come to see the weak points of the land." ¹⁰"No, my lord," they replied. "On the contrary, your servants have come to buy food. ¹¹All of us are sons of the same man. We are honest men; your servants have never been spies." ¹²But he answered them: "Not so! It is the weak points of the land that you have come to see." ¹³"We your servants," they said, "are twelve brothers, sons of a certain man in Canaan; but the youngest one is at present with our father, and the other one is no more." ¹⁴"It is just as I said," Joseph persisted; "you are spies. ¹⁵This is how you shall be tested: I swear by the life of Pharaoh that you shall not leave here unless your youngest brother comes here. ¹⁶So send one of your number to get your brother, while the rest

continue

42:1-38 The brothers' first journey to Egypt

Jacob and his family feel the effects of the famine, suffering from hunger and also from inability to find a solution for their desperate situation. It is Jacob who suggests a way out of their difficulty: he sends them to Egypt for rations. Ironically, he is sending them to their brother Joseph, just as he sent Joseph to his brothers long ago, precipitating his sale into slavery. He has resumed his place at the head of his family, after suffering the heartbreaking loss of his son Joseph. In fact, on account of losing Joseph he does not permit Benjamin to go with his brothers to Egypt because he does not want to risk losing the only living son of his beloved Rachel. The ten brothers travel together because there is safety in numbers, and perhaps because they hope to secure more rations for the family.

In verse 6 the ten brothers come to Joseph and pay the appropriate homage to him. They bow low just as his boyhood dream predicted. Joseph recognizes them immediately, but does not identify himself to them. On the contrary, he treats them harshly, remembering his dreams and their mocking reaction to them. His accusation that they are spies is plausible because the route into Egypt from Canaan was vulnerable to attack. In their effort to convince him that they are not spies they begin to give him information about the family. The more they tell him, the more he persists in his accusation: his memories of their abuse urge him to be harsh, while his eagerness for news of his father and brother presses him to learn as much as possible from his brothers.

His solution is to impose a series of tests; the first of these is for one brother to go home and bring the youngest while the others wait in prison for them to return. Three days later he changes his orders, sending all of them home with food for their families. In this way he assures himself that Jacob and Benjamin will not go hungry. The brothers, still in Joseph's presence, interpret his orders as punishment for their earlier abusive treatment of him, but they do not recognize him.

Reuben's chastisement of the others in verse 22 touches Joseph: he realizes that Reuben tried to save him from the brothers' plot. He leaves the room rather than weep in their presence and divulge his identity. Joseph takes the second-oldest, Simeon, hostage rather than Reuben, the oldest, in light of Reuben's earlier efforts to save him. He arranges for the others to have grain, money, and provisions for the return trip; then the brothers begin their journey home.

They are unaware that their money has been returned until one of them opens his bag and finds it (v. 28). Then the brothers realize that their situation is extremely precarious: they must eventually return to Egypt with their brother Benjamin in order to rescue Simeon and procure more grain, but they risk being accused of stealing the money once they arrive there. The brothers find themselves at the mercy of God in their predicament. Joseph's reason for ordering the money to be returned is not given: does he mean for the brothers to have the money because it is theirs? Or does he mean to give them grief? Or is he imposing another test on them?

Once back home, the brothers tell their father about their experiences in Egypt. Ironically they report that they called themselves honest men, still not realizing that they were speaking to the brother they tried to destroy. Then they discover that all their money has been returned, not just one person's. Their father is particularly stricken, fearing that he will lose his youngest son Benjamin to Egypt. Even though Reuben suggests that his own two sons could be ransom for Benjamin, Jacob will not agree to let Benjamin go. This is the last time the narrative depicts Reuben taking leadership in his position as firstborn. From now on it is Judah who assumes responsibility for his brothers. Judah is Jacob's fourth son; the first three (Reuben, Simeon, and Levi) have disgraced themselves: Simeon and Levi in the destruction of Shechem in chapter 34, and Reuben by sleeping with his father's concubine in 35:22.

of you stay here under arrest. Thus will your words be tested for their truth; if they are untrue, as Pharaoh lives, you are spies!" [17]With that, he locked them up in the guardhouse for three days.

[18]On the third day Joseph said to them: "Do this, and you shall live; for I am a God-fearing man. [19]If you are honest men, let one of your brothers be confined in this prison, while the rest of you go and take home grain for your starving families. [20]But you must bring me your youngest brother. Your words will thus be verified, and you will not die." To this they agreed. [21]To one another, however, they said: "Truly we are being punished because of our brother. We saw the anguish of his heart when he pleaded with us, yet we would not listen. That is why this anguish has now come upon us." [22]Then Reuben responded, "Did I not tell you, 'Do no wrong to the boy'? But you would not listen! Now comes the reckoning for his blood." [23]They did not know, of course, that Joseph understood what they said, since he spoke with them through an interpreter. [24]But turning away from them, he wept. When he was able to speak to them again, he took Simeon from among them and bound him before their eyes. [25]Then Joseph gave orders to have their containers filled with grain, their money replaced in each one's sack, and provisions given them for their journey. After this had been done for them, [26]they loaded their donkeys with the grain and departed.

[27]At the night encampment, when one of them opened his bag to give his donkey some fodder, he saw his money there in the mouth of his bag. [28]He cried out to his brothers, "My money has been returned! Here it is in my bag!" At that their hearts sank. Trembling, they asked one another, "What is this that God has done to us?"

[29]When they got back to their father Jacob in the land of Canaan, they told him all that had happened to them. [30]"The man who is lord of the land," they said, "spoke to us harshly and put us in custody on the grounds that we were spying on the land. [31]But we said to him: 'We are honest

continue

men; we have never been spies. ³²We are twelve brothers, sons of the same father; but one is no more, and the youngest one is now with our father in the land of Canaan.' ³³Then the man who is lord of the land said to us: 'This is how I will know if you are honest men: leave one of your brothers with me, then take grain for your starving families and go. ³⁴When you bring me your youngest brother, and I know that you are not spies but honest men, I will restore your brother to you, and you may move about freely in the land.'"

³⁵When they were emptying their sacks, there in each one's sack was his moneybag! At the sight of their moneybags, they and their father were afraid. ³⁶Their father Jacob said to them: "Must you make me childless? Joseph is no more, Simeon is no more, and now you would take Benjamin away! All these things have happened to me!" ³⁷Then Reuben told his father: "You may kill my own two sons if I do not return him to you! Put him in my care, and I will bring him back to you." ³⁸But Jacob replied: "My son shall not go down with you. Now that his brother is dead, he is the only one left. If some disaster should befall him on the journey you must make, you would send my white head down to Sheol in grief."

CHAPTER 43

The Second Journey to Egypt

¹Now the famine in the land grew severe. ²So when they had used up all the grain they had brought from Egypt, their father said to them, "Go back and buy us a little more food." ³But Judah replied: "The man strictly warned us, 'You shall not see me unless your brother is with you.' ⁴If you are willing to let our brother go with us, we will go down to buy food for you. ⁵But if you are not willing, we will not go down, because the man told us, 'You shall not see me unless your brother is with you.'" ⁶Israel demanded, "Why did you bring this trouble on me by telling the man that you had another brother?" ⁷They an-

continue

43:1-34 The second journey to Egypt

The family gradually uses all the rations the brothers brought home from Egypt, and Jacob suggests a second trip to buy more food for them. Judah reminds him of the terms: Benjamin must go with them, or they will all be condemned as spies. Jacob now realizes how precarious their situation is: the brothers must take Benjamin with them if they return to Egypt. Jacob is distraught that his sons gave the Egyptian official so much information about their family, but they reply that he pressured them into it, and they complied, not knowing how the information would be used against them. Judah pleads with his father that this is their one hope of survival, because only in Egypt will they be able to find food for their families. Judah makes another offer to his father, commenting that they are wasting precious time by debating the inevitable. He pledges that, if the mission fails, he personally will assume the responsibility.

Jacob finally and reluctantly relents in verse 11. He tells his sons to take gifts with them; ironically they include the same items (balm, gum, and resin) the Ishmaelite traders had with them when they bought Joseph from his brothers in 37:25. He also advises them to take double the amount of money that was returned to them, on the chance that it was mistakenly placed in their bags. He sends Benjamin with them as well, calling on the ancient name of God to protect all of them, in the hope that both Benjamin and Simeon will be allowed to return to him. He expresses his own resignation to the possibility of not seeing either of his two sons again. The brothers make the necessary arrangements, taking along twice the amount of money they owed for the first provisions, and taking their brother Benjamin with them.

In verse 15 the brothers arrive in Joseph's house. When he sees Benjamin with them, he arranges a banquet. His steward makes the arrangements and brings the brothers into the house for the banquet, but they suspect a trap. The narrative describes the reason for their fright: they expect to be enslaved as punishment for stealing the money. In an effort to swered: "The man kept asking about us and our family: 'Is your father still living? Do you have another brother?' We answered him accordingly. How could we know that he would say, 'Bring your brother down here'?"

[8]Then Judah urged his father Israel: "Let the boy go with me, that we may be off and on our way if you and we and our children are to keep from starving to death. [9]I myself will serve as a guarantee for him. You can hold me responsible for him. If I fail to bring him back and set him before you, I will bear the blame before you forever. [10]Had we not delayed, we could have been there and back twice by now!"

[11]Israel their father then told them: "If it must be so, then do this: Put some of the land's best products in your baggage and take them down to the man as gifts: some balm and honey, gum and resin, and pistachios and almonds. [12]Also take double the money along, for you must return the amount that was put back in the mouths of your bags; it may have been a mistake. [13]Take your brother, too, and be off on your way back to the man. [14]May God Almighty grant you mercy in the presence of the man, so that he may let your other brother go, as well as Benjamin. As for me, if I am to suffer bereavement, I shall suffer it."

[15]So the men took those gifts and double the money and Benjamin. They made their way down to Egypt and presented themselves before Joseph. [16]When Joseph saw them and Benjamin, he told his steward, "Take the men into the house, and have an animal slaughtered and prepared, for they are to dine with me at noon." [17]Doing as Joseph had ordered, the steward conducted the men to Joseph's house. [18]But they became apprehensive when they were led to his house. "It must be," they thought, "on account of the money put back in our bags the first time, that we are taken inside—in order to attack us and take our donkeys and seize us as slaves." [19]So they went up to Joseph's steward and talked to him at the entrance of the house. [20]"If you please, sir," they said, "we came down here once before to buy food. [21]But when we arrived at a night's encampment and opened our bags, there was each man's money in the mouth of his bag—our money in the full amount! We have now brought it back. [22]We have brought other money to buy food. We do not know who put our money in our bags." [23]He replied, "Calm down! Do not fear! Your God and the God of your father must have put treasure in your bags for you. As for your money, I received it." With that, he led Simeon out to them.

[24]The steward then brought the men inside Joseph's house. He gave them water to wash their feet, and gave fodder to their donkeys. [25]Then they set out their gifts to await Joseph's arrival at noon, for they had heard that they were to dine there. [26]When Joseph came home, they presented him with the gifts they had brought inside, while they bowed down before him to the ground. [27]After inquiring how they were, he asked them, "And how is your aged father, of whom you spoke? Is he still alive?" [28]"Your servant our father is still alive and doing well," they said, as they knelt and bowed down. [29]Then Joseph looked up and saw Benjamin, his brother, the son of his mother. He asked, "Is this your youngest brother, of whom you told me?" Then he said to him, "May God be gracious to you, my son!" [30]With that, Joseph hurried out, for he was so overcome with affection for his brother that he was on the verge of tears. So he went into a private room and wept there.

[31]After washing his face, he reappeared and, now having collected himself, gave the order, "Serve the meal." [32]It was served separately to him, to the brothers, and to the Egyptians who partook of his board. Egyptians may not eat with Hebrews; that is abhorrent to them. [33]When they were seated before him according to their age, from the oldest to the youngest, they looked at one another in amazement; [34]and as portions were brought to them from Joseph's table, Benjamin's portion was five times as large as anyone else's. So they drank freely and made merry with him.

continue

CHAPTER 44

Final Test

[1]Then Joseph commanded his steward: "Fill the men's bags with as much food as they can carry, and put each man's money in the mouth of his bag. [2]In the mouth of the youngest one's bag put also my silver goblet, together with the money for his grain." The steward did as Joseph said. [3]At daybreak the men and their donkeys were sent off. [4]They had not gone far out of the city when Joseph said to his steward: "Go at once after the men! When you overtake them, say to them, 'Why did you repay good with evil? Why did you steal my silver goblet? [5]Is it not the very one from which my master drinks and which he uses for divination? What you have done is wrong.'"

[6]When the steward overtook them and repeated these words to them, [7]they said to him: "Why does my lord say such things? Far be it from your servants to do such a thing! [8]We even brought back to you from the land of Canaan the money that we found in the mouths of our bags. How could we steal silver or gold from your master's house? [9]If any of your servants is found to have the goblet, he shall die, and as for the rest of us, we shall become my lord's slaves." [10]But he replied, "Now what you propose is fair enough, but only the one who is found to have it shall become my slave, and the rest of you can go free." [11]Then each of them quickly lowered his bag to the ground and opened it; [12]and when a search was made, starting with the oldest and ending with the youngest, the goblet turned up in Benjamin's bag. [13]At this, they tore their garments. Then, when each man had loaded his donkey again, they returned to the city.

[14]When Judah and his brothers entered Joseph's house, he was still there; so they flung themselves on the ground before him. [15]"How could you do such a thing?" Joseph asked them. "Did you not know that such a man as I could discern by divination what happened?" [16]Judah replied: "What can we say to my lord? How can we plead

continue

forestall what they fear is inevitable they immediately explain to the chief steward that they did not, in fact, steal the money on their first trip to Egypt, but it was put back into their bags without their knowing. The chief steward then assures them they have nothing to fear; their God is behind what happened. He then brings their brother Simeon to them and treats the brothers hospitably while they wait for the arrival of their host.

When Joseph comes in, they bow down to him as they did before, and as Joseph's dream predicted. He inquires about their father, using the Hebrew word "shalom" or "wholeness," the expression for health and well-being, in verses 27-28. Joseph then acknowledges Benjamin, but still does not identify himself to his brothers. Then his feelings wash over him, and he leaves the room rather than weep in his brothers' presence. When he returns he orders the meal served. He hosts a feast for his brothers; earlier they enjoyed a meal after throwing him into the cistern (37:25). They are served separately according to the Egyptian custom of not eating with foreigners. (They were considered unclean because they were shepherds.) The brothers are seated according to age, and are amazed at the gracious hospitality of their host. Benjamin receives portions five times larger than the other brothers, but the reason is not given: is Joseph heaping special treatment on his full brother because he is so happy to see him? Or is he watching for signs of envy from his other brothers, like their envy of him when they were young?

44:1-34 The final test

Joseph has still not identified himself to his brothers. He instructs his steward to pack the men's bags with provisions as they prepare to start on their journey home. In addition, the money is to be put back in their bags, and Joseph's own silver goblet is to be packed in Benjamin's bag. The silver goblet reminds us that the brothers originally sold Joseph for twenty pieces of silver; now he plants a silver vessel in the bag of Benjamin, who had nothing to do with the brothers' earlier abuse of Joseph. His orders are carried out, and early in the morning the party begins the journey home. Very soon after they depart, Joseph sends his steward after the men, to accuse them of stealing the goblet. The steward is not to refer explicitly to the goblet, but only to make an inexact accusation, to heighten the brothers' anxiety.

In verse 7 the brothers are aghast at the steward's accusation. Judah speaks for them all, protesting that they demonstrated their honesty by returning the money and questioning how he could accuse them of stealing something else. He offers to allow the guilty one to be killed, and all the rest of them will become slaves. This spontaneous protestation comes from his own conviction that his brothers are innocent, from the wariness they all experience after the previous incident with the money, and also from his eagerness to resolve the matter as quickly as possible. Judah's response is reminiscent of Jacob's assertion to Laban when he was accused of stealing the household gods in 31:30-35. But the steward insists that only the guilty one will be enslaved, and no one will be killed.

The brothers open their bags one after another, beginning with the oldest (v. 11). This procedure encourages the brothers, as one bag after another proves not to have the missing vessel. But for the reader, who knows the vessel is in the youngest brother's bag, the suspense mounts as his turn comes closer and closer. When the vessel is found in Benjamin's bag, the brothers are dumbstruck. They tear their clothes, reminiscent of their father's action when he received Joseph's bloodstained garment (37:34). For the third time they go to the city.

When they reach Joseph's house in verse 14, they prostrate themselves again, but this time the narrative uses the intensive form of the verb, expressing the brothers' sense of hopelessness that they will ever be exonerated. Joseph speaks harshly to them, accusing them and wondering how they could do such a thing: do they not realize he knows what happened because of his special powers? Judah, the spokesperson, speaks from the depth of his

or how try to prove our innocence? God has uncovered your servants' guilt. Here we are, then, the slaves of my lord—the rest of us no less than the one in whose possession the goblet was found." [17]Joseph said, "Far be it from me to act thus! Only the one in whose possession the goblet was found shall become my slave; the rest of you may go back unharmed to your father."

[18]Judah then stepped up to him and said: "I beg you, my lord, let your servant appeal to my lord, and do not become angry with your servant, for you are the equal of Pharaoh. [19]My lord asked his servants, 'Have you a father, or another brother?' [20]So we said to my lord, 'We have an aged father, and a younger brother, the child of his old age. This one's full brother is dead, and since he is the only one by his mother who is left, his father is devoted to him.' [21]Then you told your servants, 'Bring him down to me that I might see him.' [22]We replied to my lord, 'The boy cannot leave his father; his father would die if he left him.' [23]But you told your servants, 'Unless your youngest brother comes down with you, you shall not see me again.' [24]When we returned to your servant my father, we reported to him the words of my lord.

[25]"Later, our father said, 'Go back and buy some food for us.' [26]So we reminded him, 'We cannot go down there; only if our youngest brother is with us can we go, for we may not see the man if our youngest brother is not with us.' [27]Then your servant my father said to us, 'As you know, my wife bore me two sons. [28]One of them, however, has gone away from me, and I said, "He must have been torn to pieces by wild beasts!" I have not seen him since. [29]If you take this one away from me too, and a disaster befalls him, you will send my white head down to Sheol in grief.'

[30]"So now, if the boy is not with us when I go back to your servant my father, whose very life is bound up with his, he will die as soon as he sees that the boy is missing; [31]and your servants will thus send the white head of your servant our father down to Sheol in grief. [32]Besides, I, your

continue

servant, have guaranteed the boy's safety for my father by saying, 'If I fail to bring him back to you, father, I will bear the blame before you forever.' ³³So now let me, your servant, remain in place of the boy as the slave of my lord, and let the boy go back with his brothers. ³⁴How could I go back to my father if the boy were not with me? I could not bear to see the anguish that would overcome my father."

despair, wondering how the brothers can possibly break free of the misunderstandings and accusations they have suffered since they first arrived in Egypt. Again he asserts that all the brothers will stand together and accept the punishment of slavery. Joseph insists that only the guilty one will be punished, as his steward had specified.

Then Judah recounts the entire story of the brothers' first arrival in Egypt, the pain and grief their father suffered over the loss of Rachel and over the possible loss of Rachel's only remaining son, the brothers' concern that their father will die of grief if Benjamin does not return to him, and even his own pledge to Jacob that he will assume the guilt if anything happens to Benjamin. With these words Judah brings the story back to its beginning: the one who sold Joseph into slavery is now willing to accept slavery himself rather than devastate their father.

EXPLORING LESSON FOUR

1. a) What is Joseph's special gift for which he gives God credit (40:4b-8)?

_____

_____

_____

   b) What gifts, skills, or talents have you received for which you give God credit?

_____

_____

_____

2. What is Joseph's interpretation of Pharaoh's dream (41:1-32)?

_____

_____

_____

_____

_____

3. How does Joseph's conversation with Pharaoh indicate that Joseph's wisdom goes far beyond simply interpreting dreams (41:33-36)?

_____

_____

_____

_____

_____

4. When Pharaoh invests Joseph with special garments, it represents a new dignity for Joseph (41:40-43). Where else in the Joseph saga has clothing been important? (See 37:3; 37:31-35; 38:18-19; 39:11-15.)

_____

_____

_____

_____

_____

5. What is it about Joseph's marriage that contrasts with both Isaac's and Jacob's marriages (41:50-52)? (See 24:1-4; 27:46-28:2.)

_____

_____

_____

_____

6. When Joseph's brothers arrive in Egypt to purchase grain the first time, what do they do to fulfill the prophetic nature of Joseph's dreams (42:6)? (See 37:5-11.)

_____

_____

_____

_____

7. What do you think motivates Joseph to secretly place his brothers' payments for the grain back into their sacks (42:25-29)?

_____

_____

_____

_____

8. How does the placing of the goblet in Benjamin's bag bring the story of Joseph's reunion with his brothers to its most critical stage (44:1-34)?

_____

_____

_____

_____

9. What elements of the Joseph story have captured your imagination most?

_____

_____

_____

_____

_____

CLOSING PRAYER

Prayer

Joseph collected grain like the sands of the sea,
so much that at last he stopped measuring it,
for it was beyond measure.   (Gen 41:49)

O God who filled Joseph with wisdom, share with us
the wisdom we need. Help us to recognize our blessings
and to seek your direction in how to use our gifts. We
pray for the ability to seize opportunities and offer our
own gifts, especially . . .

LESSON FIVE

Genesis 45–50

Begin your personal study and group discussion with a simple and sincere prayer such as:

Prayer

God of my ancestors in faith, open my eyes and ears and heart as I reflect on these people whom you called centuries ago.

Read the Bible text of Genesis 45–50 found in the outside columns of pages 76–86, highlighting what stands out to you.

Read the accompanying commentary to add to your understanding.

Respond to the questions on pages 87–88, Exploring Lesson Five.

The Closing Prayer on page 89 is for your personal use and may be used at the end of group discussion.

CHAPTER 45

The Truth Revealed

¹Joseph could no longer restrain himself in the presence of all his attendants, so he cried out, "Have everyone withdraw from me!" So no one attended him when he made himself known to his brothers. ²But his sobs were so loud that the Egyptians heard him, and so the news reached Pharaoh's house. ³"I am Joseph," he said to his brothers. "Is my father still alive?" But his brothers could give him no answer, so dumbfounded were they at him.

⁴"Come closer to me," Joseph told his brothers. When they had done so, he said: "I am your brother Joseph, whom you sold into Egypt. ⁵But now do not be distressed, and do not be angry with yourselves for having sold me here. It was really for the sake of saving lives that God sent me here ahead of you. ⁶The famine has been in the land for two years now, and for five more years cultivation will yield no harvest. ⁷God, therefore, sent me on ahead of you to ensure for you a remnant on earth and to save your lives in an extraordinary deliverance. ⁸So it was not really you but God who had me come here; and he has made me a father to Pharaoh, lord of all his household, and ruler over the whole land of Egypt.

⁹"Hurry back, then, to my father and tell him: 'Thus says your son Joseph: God has made me lord of all Egypt; come down to me without delay. ¹⁰You can settle in the region of Goshen, where you will be near me—you and your children and children's children, your flocks and herds, and everything that you own. ¹¹I will provide for you there in the five years of famine that lie ahead, so that you and your household and all that are yours will not suffer want.' ¹²Surely, you can see for yourselves, and Benjamin can see for himself, that it is I who am speaking to you. ¹³Tell my father all about my high position in Egypt and all that you have seen. But hurry and bring my father down here." ¹⁴Then he threw his arms around his brother Benjamin and wept on his shoulder. ¹⁵Joseph then

continue

45:1-28 Joseph reveals himself to his brothers

Judah's words touch Joseph so deeply that he can no longer hide his identity from his brothers. He dismisses his attendants, then weeps for the third time. But this time he stays with his brothers, says simply, "I am Joseph," then inquires about his father (45:3). The image of his father's grief over the loss of his two sons by Rachel ultimately moves Joseph to identify himself to his brothers. The brothers are speechless. Joseph repeats his identity, adding that he is the one they sold into slavery. His words highlight both his identity and his former strained relationship with them. He then explains that, even though the brothers acted sinfully, everything has happened through God's care, to pave the way for them in Egypt. He sends them back to their father with instructions to bring him back to Egypt, where he will have enough fertile land for his family, livestock, and all his possessions, so they can survive the five years of famine that remain. They will live in Goshen, in the northeastern part of Egypt, where the land is ideal for cattle grazing. Joseph and Benjamin embrace (v. 14), then Joseph embraces each of his other brothers. Finally they are able to talk to him after his shocking revelation, and after all the years of strained relationships (37:15).

In verse 16 Pharaoh himself sends greetings to Joseph's brothers, and encourages Joseph to send for his father and the entire family. He repeats the offer in a formal order. Joseph gives his brothers provisions for their travel; to Benjamin he gives extra gifts, and sends gifts and provisions to his father as well. His final word is puzzling; the Hebrew text can mean, "Do not fear for your safety" or "Do not recriminate."

When Jacob hears that Joseph is not only alive, but a ruler of Egypt, it is his turn to be incredulous (v. 26). When he sees all the provisions Joseph has sent for their journey, he determines to go to Egypt to see Joseph.

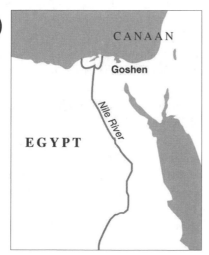

46:1–47:12 Jacob's migration to Egypt

Jacob leaves his home, most likely in Hebron (37:14) and goes first to Beer-sheba where he lived with his parents before traveling to Haran (28:10), and where his father Isaac received the Lord's blessing (26:23-25). The connection with Isaac seems to be his reason for going to that place, as the narrative specifies that he offers sacrifices to "the God of his father Isaac" (v. 1). There he has a vision in which God calls to him and he responds, "Here I am," expressing his readiness to do whatever God asks of him. God reassures him, repeats the promise of a great nation, and promises to bring him back after Joseph closes Jacob's eyes in death. The divine promises provide a clue as to why Jacob visits the shrine: he is leaving this land

kissed all his brothers and wept over them; and only then were his brothers able to talk with him.

16The news reached Pharaoh's house: "Joseph's brothers have come." Pharaoh and his officials were pleased. 17So Pharaoh told Joseph: "Say to your brothers: 'This is what you shall do: Load up your animals and go without delay to the land of Canaan. 18There get your father and your households, and then come to me; I will assign you the best land in Egypt, where you will live off the fat of the land.' 19Instruct them further: 'Do this. Take wagons from the land of Egypt for your children and your wives and bring your father back here. 20Do not be concerned about your belongings, for the best in the whole land of Egypt shall be yours.'"

21The sons of Israel acted accordingly. Joseph gave them the wagons, as Pharaoh had ordered, and he supplied them with provisions for the journey. 22He also gave to each of them a set of clothes, but to Benjamin he gave three hundred shekels of silver and five sets of clothes. 23Moreover, what he sent to his father was ten donkeys loaded with the finest products of Egypt and another ten loaded with grain and bread and provisions for his father's journey. 24As he sent his brothers on their way, he told them, "Do not quarrel on the way."

25So they went up from Egypt and came to the land of Canaan, to their father Jacob. 26When they told him, "Joseph is still alive—in fact, it is he who is governing all the land of Egypt," he was unmoved, for he did not believe them. 27But when they recounted to him all that Joseph had told them, and when he saw the wagons that Joseph had sent to transport him, the spirit of their father Jacob came to life. 28"Enough," said Israel. "My son Joseph is still alive! I must go and see him before I die."

CHAPTER 46

Migration to Egypt

1Israel set out with all that was his. When he arrived at Beer-sheba, he offered sacrifices to the God of his father Isaac. 2There God, speaking to Israel in a vision by night, called: Jacob! Jacob!

continue

He answered, "Here I am." ³Then he said: I am God, the God of your father. Do not be afraid to go down to Egypt, for there I will make you a great nation. ⁴I will go down to Egypt with you and I will also bring you back here, after Joseph has closed your eyes.

⁵So Jacob departed from Beer-sheba, and the sons of Israel put their father and their wives and children on the wagons that Pharaoh had sent to transport him. ⁶They took with them their livestock and the possessions they had acquired in the land of Canaan. So Jacob and all his descendants came to Egypt. ⁷His sons and his grandsons, his daughters and his granddaughters—all his descendants—he took with him to Egypt.

⁸These are the names of the Israelites, Jacob and his children, who came to Egypt.

Reuben, Jacob's firstborn, ⁹and the sons of Reuben: Hanoch, Pallu, Hezron, and Carmi. ¹⁰The sons of Simeon: Jemuel, Jamin, Ohad, Jachin, Zohar, and Shaul, son of a Canaanite woman. ¹¹The sons of Levi: Gershon, Kohath, and Merari. ¹²The sons of Judah: Er, Onan, Shelah, Perez, and Zerah—but Er and Onan had died in the land of Canaan; and the sons of Perez were Hezron and Hamul. ¹³The sons of Issachar: Tola, Puah, Jashub, and Shimron. ¹⁴The sons of Zebulun: Sered, Elon, and Jahleel. ¹⁵These were the sons whom Leah bore to Jacob in Paddan-aram, along with his daughter Dinah—thirty-three persons in all, sons and daughters.

¹⁶The sons of Gad: Zephon, Haggi, Shuni, Ezbon, Eri, Arod, and Areli. ¹⁷The sons of Asher: Imnah, Ishvah, Ishvi, and Beriah, with their sister Serah; and the sons of Beriah: Heber and Malchiel. ¹⁸These are the children of Zilpah, whom Laban had given to his daughter Leah; these she bore to Jacob—sixteen persons in all.

¹⁹The sons of Jacob's wife Rachel: Joseph and Benjamin. ²⁰In the land of Egypt Joseph became the father of Manasseh and Ephraim, whom Asenath, daughter of Potiphera, priest of Heliopolis, bore to him. ²¹The sons of Benjamin: Bela, Becher, Ashbel, Gera, Naaman, Ahiram, Shupham,

Hupham, and Ard. ²²These are the sons whom Rachel bore to Jacob—fourteen persons in all.

²³The sons of Dan: Hushim. ²⁴The sons of Naphtali: Jahzeel, Guni, Jezer, and Shillem. ²⁵These are the sons of Bilhah, whom Laban had given to his daughter Rachel; these she bore to Jacob—seven persons in all.

²⁶Jacob's people who came to Egypt—his direct descendants, not counting the wives of Jacob's sons—numbered sixty-six persons in all. ²⁷Together with Joseph's sons who were born to him in Egypt—two persons—all the people comprising the household of Jacob who had come to Egypt amounted to seventy persons in all.

²⁸Israel had sent Judah ahead to Joseph, so that he might meet him in Goshen. On his arrival in the region of Goshen, ²⁹Joseph prepared his chariot and went up to meet his father Israel in Goshen. As soon as Israel made his appearance, Joseph threw his arms around him and wept a long time on his shoulder. ³⁰And Israel said to Joseph, "At last I can die, now that I have seen for myself that you are still alive."

³¹Joseph then said to his brothers and his father's household: "I will go up and inform Pharaoh, telling him: 'My brothers and my father's household, whose home is in the land of Canaan, have come to me. ³²The men are shepherds, having been owners of livestock; and they have brought with them their flocks and herds, as well as everything else they own.' ³³So when Pharaoh summons you and asks what your occupation is, ³⁴you must answer, 'We your servants, like our ancestors, have been owners of livestock from our youth until now,' in order that you may stay in the region of Goshen, since all shepherds are abhorrent to the Egyptians."

CHAPTER 47

Settlement in Goshen

¹Joseph went and told Pharaoh, "My father and my brothers have come from the land of Canaan, with their flocks and herds and everything else they own; and they are now in the region of Goshen." ²He then presented to Pharaoh five of

continue

that has been promised to him, and the future is full of uncertainties. The divine reassurance convinces him that his decision to go to Egypt is a sound one.

It was the custom (and is still so in Jewish families) for the oldest son to close his father's eyes when he dies. Joseph is Jacob's first son by his beloved wife Rachel; here he receives a divine promise that Joseph will be with him at the moment of his death (see 49:33–50:1).

A genealogical list follows in verses 8-27, enumerating all those who travel with Jacob to Egypt. The list is arranged according to Jacob's twelve sons and one daughter by their respective mothers. The list includes Er and Onan, Judah's two deceased sons; it also includes Joseph along with his two sons who were born in Egypt. The total number given in verse 26 is sixty-six, not counting Er and Onan, who had already died, or Joseph's two sons who were born in Egypt, or Leah's daughter Dinah, even though she is listed in the genealogy. Then verse 27 gives the number seventy, after adding Joseph's two sons to the count.

Much effort has been made to reconcile these numbers, which have several problematic aspects in addition to the puzzling difference in the totals. For example, the list of Benjamin's sons differs here from corresponding lists in Numbers 26:38-40; 1 Chronicles 7:6; and 8:1-2; each of which is slightly different from the others. Quite possibly the significance of the number seventy, rather than the exact count, is the important aspect of it, as seventy is considered ten times the perfect number seven. (In Exod 1:5, the number of Jacob's family who migrate to Egypt is given as seventy.) The genealogy solemnly testifies that the entire family goes to Egypt, as Genesis 15:13 predicts. The list marks the end of the ancestral period in the land, and provides a transition to the next stage of the family story.

As the party approaches Goshen where they will live, Jacob sends Judah ahead to alert Joseph of their arrival. Thus Judah, who suggested selling Joseph and thus caused his separation from his father, now arranges their reunion. Joseph hurries out to meet his father

his brothers whom he had selected from their full number. ³When Pharaoh asked them, "What is your occupation?" they answered, "We, your servants, like our ancestors, are shepherds. ⁴We have come," they continued, "in order to sojourn in this land, for there is no pasture for your servants' flocks, because the famine has been severe in the land of Canaan. So now please let your servants settle in the region of Goshen." ⁵Pharaoh said to Joseph, "Now that your father and your brothers have come to you, ⁶the land of Egypt is at your disposal; settle your father and brothers in the pick of the land. Let them settle in the region of Goshen. And if you know of capable men among them, put them in charge of my livestock." ⁷Then Joseph brought his father Jacob and presented him to Pharaoh. And Jacob blessed Pharaoh. ⁸Then Pharaoh asked Jacob, "How many years have you lived?" ⁹Jacob replied: "The years I have lived as a wayfarer amount to a hundred and thirty. Few and hard have been these years of my life, and they do not compare with the years that my ancestors lived as wayfarers." ¹⁰Then Jacob blessed Pharaoh and withdrew from his presence.

¹¹Joseph settled his father and brothers and gave them a holding in Egypt on the pick of the land, in the region of Rameses, as Pharaoh had ordered. ¹²And Joseph provided food for his father and brothers and his father's whole household, down to the youngest.

continue

as the caravan approaches. This time it is he who is overcome; his father expresses his sentiment that now that he has seen Joseph, his life is complete (v. 30). Joseph explains that he will formally notify Pharaoh of his family's arrival, and coaches his brothers that they are to identify themselves as owners of livestock like the Egyptians. This statement is puzzling in view of his final remark, "all shepherds are abhorrent to the Egyptians."

Joseph takes several of his brothers with him when he formally notifies Pharaoh of his

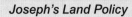

Joseph's Land Policy

¹³Since there was no food in all the land because of the extreme severity of the famine, and the lands of Egypt and Canaan were languishing from hunger, ¹⁴Joseph gathered in, as payment for the grain that they were buying, all the money that was to be found in Egypt and Canaan, and he put it in Pharaoh's house. ¹⁵When all the money in Egypt and Canaan was spent, all the Egyptians came to Joseph, pleading, "Give us food! Why should we perish in front of you? For our money is gone." ¹⁶"Give me your livestock if your money is gone," replied Joseph. "I will give you food in return for your livestock." ¹⁷So they brought their livestock to Joseph, and he gave them food in exchange for their horses, their flocks of sheep and herds of cattle, and their donkeys. Thus he supplied them with food in exchange for all their livestock in that year. ¹⁸That year ended, and they came to him in the next one and said: "We cannot hide from my lord that, with our money spent and our livestock made over to my lord, there is nothing left to put at my lord's disposal except our bodies and our land. ¹⁹Why should we and our land perish before your very eyes? Take us and our land in exchange for food, and we will become Pharaoh's slaves and our land his property; only give us seed, that we may survive and not perish, and that our land may not turn into a waste."

²⁰So Joseph acquired all the land of Egypt for Pharaoh. Each of the Egyptians sold his field, since the famine weighed heavily upon them. Thus the land passed over to Pharaoh, ²¹and the people were reduced to slavery, from one end of Egypt's territory to the other. ²²Only the priests' lands Joseph did not acquire. Since the priests had a fixed allowance from Pharaoh and lived off the allowance Pharaoh had granted them, they did not have to sell their land.

²³Joseph told the people: "Now that I have acquired you and your land for Pharaoh, here is your seed for sowing the land. ²⁴But when the harvest is in, you must give a fifth of it to Pharaoh,

continue

family's arrival in 47:1. They state their occupation as shepherds and explain that they have come to stay on a temporary basis because of the famine. Pharaoh gives his formal approval to Joseph, authorizing them to stay in Goshen and serve as royal officers. This designation affords them legal status to which they would not otherwise be entitled as aliens. The approval implicitly makes Joseph responsible for the family.

The next audience is between Pharaoh and Jacob (v. 7). Pharaoh asks Jacob about his age, and his reply indicates that he has lived beyond the Egyptian ideal of 110 years. Jacob refers to himself as a wayfarer, perhaps in reference to his life as a journey, perhaps to emphasize his many travels, or perhaps to call attention to his alien status in Egypt. Joseph arranges for his family to have what they need for their stay in Egypt.

47:13-27 Joseph's land policy

The narrative picks up the story from 41:57 when the famine begins to affect everyone. The situation is dire, and Joseph takes drastic steps to keep the people from starving. First he collects all the money in the land as payment for grain, but keeps none of it for himself. Then he barters livestock for grain. When the people have no more livestock they give over their land and become slaves of the state. Thus the state comes to own all the money, livestock, land, and people except for the priests who have a special allotment from Pharaoh. Then Joseph gives the people seed to plant, with the stipulation that they give one-fifth of the crops to Pharaoh at harvest time. The people are profoundly grateful to Joseph, and readily accept the terms of the agreement. Meanwhile, Jacob's family thrives in their new home in Egypt (v. 27).

It is difficult to understand this arrangement in contemporary Western terms. In the ancient Near East, during the time of Hammurabi, a tax such as the one Joseph imposed could be as high as two-thirds. In Babylon the rate was between one-fifth and one-third. All these rates seem exorbitant to us; perhaps the narrator thought so, too, and avoided placing the responsibility for the policy on Joseph by having the people suggest enslavement. A brief note follows, that the practice became law, and was still in effect at the time the narrative was written.

By removing any moral stigma from Joseph, the narrative focuses on the wise policies Joseph introduces, portraying him as a concerned and creative administrator who takes bold action in a time of crisis, and thus saves Egypt from devastation.

47:28–48:22 Jacob's last days

When Jacob first arrives in Egypt he rejoices at the opportunity to see Joseph again before he dies; in fact, his sojourn in Egypt extends to seventeen years. This is the same as the amount of time before the two were separated (37:2), giving a sense of completion to Jacob's sojourn in Egypt. Jacob exacts a solemn oath from Joseph not to bury him in Egypt but to return his remains to the family burial place in the cave of Machpelah. Of all the ancestors, Jacob is the only one to die on alien soil. We can assume from the divine assurance to him at Beer-sheba before leaving for Egypt that Jacob was concerned about leaving the land. The divine promise highlights the importance of his being buried with his forebears in the land promised to him (46:4). Joseph swears to the agreement with the same gesture that Abraham's servant used when he agreed to go to Haran to find a wife for Isaac (24:2-9). Then Jacob bows his head in gratitude, perhaps to Joseph, perhaps to God, or perhaps to both.

Jacob's next act in preparation for death is to establish Joseph's sons as tribes. Joseph receives word in 48:1 that his father is not well. Joseph and his two sons visit his father, who is called Israel here because he is the father, not only of twelve sons, but of twelve tribes. He finds the strength to sit up in bed when his guests arrive. The next few verses are an E variation on the previous scene. Jacob recalls that at Bethel when he was starting out on his way to Haran (28:18-19), a dream established him as the keeper of the divine promise. Now he formally adopts his two grandsons as his own

while you keep four-fifths as seed for your fields and as food for yourselves and your households and as food for your children." [25]"You have saved our lives!" they answered. "We have found favor with my lord; now we will be Pharaoh's slaves." [26]Thus Joseph made it a statute for the land of Egypt, which is still in force, that a fifth of its produce should go to Pharaoh. Only the land of the priests did not pass over to Pharaoh.

Israel Blesses Ephraim and Manasseh

[27]Thus Israel settled in the land of Egypt, in the region of Goshen. There they acquired holdings, were fertile, and multiplied greatly. [28] Jacob lived in the land of Egypt for seventeen years; the span of his life came to a hundred and forty-seven years. [29]When the time approached for Israel to die, he called his son Joseph and said to him: "If it pleases you, put your hand under my thigh as a sign of your enduring fidelity to me; do not bury me in Egypt. [30]When I lie down with my ancestors, take me out of Egypt and bury me in their burial place." "I will do as you say," he replied. [31]But his father demanded, "Swear it to me!" So Joseph swore to him. Then Israel bowed at the head of the bed.

CHAPTER 48

[1]Some time afterward, Joseph was informed, "Your father is failing." So he took along with him his two sons, Manasseh and Ephraim. [2]When Jacob was told, "Your son Joseph has come to you," Israel rallied his strength and sat up in bed.

[3]Jacob then said to Joseph: "God Almighty appeared to me at Luz in the land of Canaan, and blessing me, [4]he said, 'I will make you fertile and multiply you and make you into an assembly of peoples, and I will give this land to your descendants after you as a permanent possession.' [5]So now your two sons who were born to you in the land of Egypt before I joined you here, shall be mine; Ephraim and Manasseh shall be mine as much as Reuben and Simeon are mine. [6]Progeny born to you after them shall remain yours; but their

continue

heritage shall be recorded in the names of their brothers. ⁷ I do this because, when I was returning from Paddan, your mother Rachel died, to my sorrow, during the journey in Canaan, while we were still a short distance from Ephrath; and I buried her there on the way to Ephrath [now Bethlehem]."

⁸When Israel saw Joseph's sons, he asked, "Who are these?" ⁹"They are my sons," Joseph answered his father, "whom God has given me here." "Bring them to me," said his father, "that I may bless them." ¹⁰Now Israel's eyes were dim from age; he could not see well. When Joseph brought his sons close to him, he kissed and embraced them. ¹¹Then Israel said to Joseph, "I never expected to see your face again, and now God has allowed me to see your descendants as well!"

¹²Joseph removed them from his father's knees and bowed down before him with his face to the ground. ¹³Then Joseph took the two, Ephraim with his right hand, to Israel's left, and Manasseh with his left hand, to Israel's right, and brought them up to him. ¹⁴But Israel, crossing his hands, put out his right hand and laid it on the head of Ephraim, although he was the younger, and his left hand on the head of Manasseh, although he was the firstborn. ¹⁵Then he blessed them with these words:

"May the God in whose presence
    my fathers Abraham and Isaac walked,
The God who has been my shepherd
    from my birth to this day,
¹⁶The angel who has delivered me from all
    harm,
    bless these boys
That in them my name be recalled,
    and the names of my fathers, Abraham
        and Isaac,
And they may become teeming multitudes
    upon the earth!"

¹⁷When Joseph saw that his father had laid his right hand on Ephraim's head, this seemed wrong to him; so he took hold of his father's hand, to remove it from Ephraim's head to Manasseh's, ¹⁸saying, "That is not right, father; the other one

continue

sons, thus passing the divine promises along to them.

Jacob follows a legal ritual: he formally states his intent to adopt the two boys, asks Joseph to name them, embraces them, and bows profoundly. Verse 6 suggests that Joseph has other sons as well, but Jacob adopts only the first two. Jacob's recollections of Rachel might suggest that she would have had more children if she had lived; but since she died so young Joseph's sons take the place of the children Rachel never had. He highlights his past grief and present joy, commenting that he once thought he would never see his son Joseph again, and now he sees Joseph's children.

Joseph places his sons close to Jacob to receive his blessing, with Manasseh the firstborn in a position to receive the blessing of the firstborn. At this point the text refers to Jacob by his name of Israel, focusing on his role as father of the twelve sons who become the twelve tribes of Israel. He puts his right hand on the head of his younger grandson Ephraim. Then, before blessing either grandson Israel blesses Joseph, the boys' father. When Joseph tries to reposition Israel's hands so the firstborn will receive the blessing, Israel insists that the younger will be the greater. Thus Israel establishes the younger over the older, just as he received his father Isaac's blessing before Isaac died. The blessing highlights Joseph's privileged place among his brothers, ten of whom are older than he is.

49:1-27 Jacob blesses his sons

Chapter 49 is a complex collection of poems, with sections devoted to each of Jacob's twelve sons. They are arranged in the form of a testament, that is, last words that leave a legacy for his family. Jacob alternates between speaking to the sons and speaking about them; this is awkward for modern readers but was frequent in ancient speech. Jacob first addresses Leah's six sons, then the four sons of the maids, beginning and ending with one of Bilhah's children. Finally he speaks to Joseph and Benjamin, his two youngest sons and his children by his beloved Rachel. Even though he has just adopted Joseph's two sons as his own, they are not included in this testament. In some instances Jacob's words relate to different sons' previous actions; in others the words seem to relate to the lives of the tribes after they settled in the land.

Reuben (vv. 3-4): Jacob voices his condemnation of Reuben for sleeping with Bilhah in 35:22. Historically the tribe of Reuben actually disappeared very early.

Simeon and Levi (vv. 5-7): Jacob speaks of the two together, condemning their wanton destruction of the Shechemites in chapter 34, and predicting that they will not remain together. Historically, in time the tribe of Simeon became part of Judah, and the tribe of Levi was given priestly duties rather than land.

Judah (vv. 8-12): After condemning his first three sons for their previous sins, Jacob blesses Judah with the status of firstborn in verse 8b, and assures his authority, especially in verse 10. Historically, Judah remained after the Assyrians destroyed the northern kingdom in 722, bringing to an end the ten tribes who lived in that area.

Zebulun (v. 13): Jacob addresses Zebulun, Leah's sixth son, before her fifth son. Jacob foretells that Zebulun will live by the sea. In fact, his land was inland; perhaps its inhabitants worked along the coast.

Issachar (vv. 14-15): Jacob foresees that this son's tribe will work in servitude.

Dan (vv. 16-17): Dan, whose name is related to the Hebrew word "judge," will promote justice in his tribe and will fend off his enemies.

A brief prayer for deliverance comes next. In its position after the words about Dan it reinforces the divine source of Dan's ability to judge.

Gad (v. 19): Gad will successfully wage war against his enemies. Historically, his tribe, who lived east of the Jordan River, fought against the other peoples of that area.

Asher (v. 20): Asher inhabited the fertile land along the northwestern coast. It was a rich farming area.

Naphtali (v. 21): The reference to a female, fast-moving animal that bears young is obscure.

Joseph (vv. 22-26): Jacob's words about Joseph, like those about Judah, are lengthy.

is the firstborn; lay your right hand on his head!" [19]But his father refused. "I know it, son," he said, "I know. That one too shall become a people, and he too shall be great. Nevertheless, his younger brother shall surpass him, and his descendants shall become a multitude of nations." [20]So he blessed them that day and said, "By you shall the people of Israel pronounce blessings, saying, 'God make you like Ephraim and Manasseh.'" Thus he placed Ephraim before Manasseh.

[21]Then Israel said to Joseph: "I am about to die. But God will be with you and will restore you to the land of your ancestors. [22]As for me, I give to you, as to the one above his brothers, Shechem, which I captured from the Amorites with my sword and bow."

CHAPTER 49

Jacob's Testament

[1]Jacob called his sons and said: "Gather around, that I may tell you what is to happen to you in days to come.

[2]"Assemble and listen, sons of Jacob,
  listen to Israel, your father.

[3]"You, Reuben, my firstborn,
  my strength and the first fruit of my vigor,
  excelling in rank and excelling in power!
[4]Turbulent as water, you shall no longer excel,
  for you climbed into your father's bed
  and defiled my couch to my sorrow.

[5]"Simeon and Levi, brothers indeed,
  weapons of violence are their knives.
[6]Let not my person enter their council,
  or my honor be joined with their company;
For in their fury they killed men,
  at their whim they maimed oxen.
[7]Cursed be their fury so fierce,
  and their rage so cruel!
I will scatter them in Jacob,
  disperse them throughout Israel.

[8]"You, Judah, shall your brothers praise
  —your hand on the neck of your enemies;

continue

the sons of your father shall bow down to
you.
⁹Judah is a lion's cub,
you have grown up on prey, my son.
He crouches, lies down like a lion,
like a lioness—who would dare rouse him?
¹⁰The scepter shall never depart from Judah,
or the mace from between his feet,
Until tribute comes to him,
and he receives the people's obedience.
¹¹He tethers his donkey to the vine,
his donkey's foal to the choicest stem.
In wine he washes his garments,
his robe in the blood of grapes.
¹²His eyes are darker than wine,
and his teeth are whiter than milk.

¹³"Zebulun shall dwell by the seashore;
he will be a haven for ships,
and his flank shall rest on Sidon.

¹⁴"Issachar is a rawboned donkey,
crouching between the saddlebags.
¹⁵When he saw how good a settled life was,
and how pleasant the land,
He bent his shoulder to the burden
and became a toiling serf.

¹⁶"Dan shall achieve justice for his people
as one of the tribes of Israel.
¹⁷Let Dan be a serpent by the roadside,
a horned viper by the path,
That bites the horse's heel,
so that the rider tumbles backward.

¹⁸"I long for your deliverance, O Lᴏʀᴅ!
¹⁹"Gad shall be raided by raiders,
but he shall raid at their heels.

²⁰"Asher's produce is rich,
and he shall furnish delicacies for kings.

²¹"Naphtali is a hind let loose,
which brings forth lovely fawns.

²²"Joseph is a wild colt,
a wild colt by a spring,
wild colts on a hillside.
²³Harrying him and shooting,

the archers opposed him;
²⁴But his bow remained taut,
and his arms were nimble,
By the power of the Mighty One of Jacob,
because of the Shepherd, the Rock of Israel,
²⁵The God of your father, who helps you,
God Almighty, who blesses you,
With the blessings of the heavens above,
the blessings of the abyss that crouches
below,
The blessings of breasts and womb,
²⁶the blessings of fresh grain and blossoms,
the blessings of the everlasting mountains,
the delights of the eternal hills.
May they rest on the head of Joseph,
on the brow of the prince among his
brothers.

²⁷"Benjamin is a ravenous wolf;
mornings he devours the prey,
and evenings he distributes the spoils."

Farewell and Death

²⁸All these are the twelve tribes of Israel, and this is what their father said about them, as he blessed them. To each he gave a suitable blessing. ²⁹Then he gave them this charge: "Since I am about to be gathered to my people, bury me with my ancestors in the cave that lies in the field of Ephron the Hittite, ³⁰the cave in the field of Machpelah, facing on Mamre, in the land of Canaan, the field that Abraham bought from Ephron the Hittite for a burial ground. ³¹There Abraham and his wife Sarah are buried, and so are Isaac and his wife Rebekah, and there, too, I buried Leah— ³²the field and the cave in it that had been purchased from the Hittites."

³³When Jacob had finished giving these instructions to his sons, he drew his feet into the bed, breathed his last, and was gathered to his people.

CHAPTER 50

Jacob's Funeral

¹Joseph flung himself upon his father and wept over him as he kissed him. ²Then Joseph ordered

continue

Parts are obscure; verses 25-26 promise him the blessings of children and land.

Benjamin (v. 27): Jacob predicts that this son will be a successful warrior. That depiction does not match the portrayal of the young Benjamin in Genesis. It does, however, address the strategic location of the tribe, dividing the northern tribes from Judah to the south.

49:28–50:14 Jacob's death and burial

After Jacob blesses his sons the story returns to the deathbed scene from 48:22. Jacob's final words repeat the instructions given privately to Joseph, to bury him with his family in the cave of Machpelah (47:29-31). This P version is more formal than the earlier J version. When Jacob dies, Joseph gives instructions for him to be embalmed. This was not the usual ancient Israelite custom, but it preserved Jacob's body so it could be transported back to Hebron as Jacob had requested. The people observe the period of mourning, then carry out Jacob's request, traveling in a large and solemn caravan. After they bury their father the sons all return to Egypt.

50:15-26 Final reconciliation

Now that their father is dead, the brothers fear that Joseph will exact revenge for their earlier mistreatment of him. They beg for his forgiveness, and Joseph is moved by their pleading. He answers them in words reminiscent of Jacob's when Rachel begged him for a child (30:2), reminding them that ultimately forgiveness comes from God. Then he sums up the message of the entire Joseph story, pointing out that God uses human actions, no matter how evil or inadequate, to achieve the divine purpose: in this case the survival of Jacob's family.

Then the story jumps ahead to the last days of Joseph, who assures his brothers that God will eventually take them back to the land that has been promised to them. He instructs his brothers to take his body with them when they leave Egypt (Exod 13:19). Joseph, like his father Jacob, is embalmed to preserve his body for its eventual return to the land of promise.

the physicians in his service to embalm his father. When the physicians embalmed Israel, ³they spent forty days at it, for that is the full period of embalming; and the Egyptians mourned him for seventy days. ⁴When the period of mourning was over, Joseph spoke to Pharaoh's household. "If you please, appeal to Pharaoh, saying: ⁵My father made me swear: 'I am dying. Bury me in my grave that I have prepared for myself in the land of Canaan.' So now let me go up to bury my father. Then I will come back." ⁶Pharaoh replied, "Go and bury your father, as he made you promise on oath."

⁷So Joseph went up to bury his father; and with him went all of Pharaoh's officials who were senior members of his household and all the other elders of the land of Egypt, ⁸as well as Joseph's whole household, his brothers, and his father's household; only their children and their flocks and herds were left in the region of Goshen. ⁹Chariots, too, and horsemen went up with him; it was a very imposing retinue.

¹⁰When they arrived at Goren-ha-atad, which is beyond the Jordan, they held there a very great and solemn memorial service; and Joseph observed seven days of mourning for his father. ¹¹When the Canaanites who inhabited the land saw the mourning at Goren-ha-atad, they said, "This is a solemn funeral on the part of the Egyptians!" That is why the place was named Abel-mizraim. It is beyond the Jordan.

¹²Thus Jacob's sons did for him as he had instructed them. ¹³They carried him to the land of Canaan and buried him in the cave in the field of Machpelah, facing on Mamre, the field that Abraham had bought for a burial ground from Ephron the Hittite.

¹⁴After Joseph had buried his father he returned to Egypt, together with his brothers and all who had gone up with him for the burial of his father.

Plea for Forgiveness

¹⁵Now that their father was dead, Joseph's brothers became fearful and thought, "Suppose Joseph has been nursing a grudge against us and

continue

now most certainly will pay us back in full for all the wrong we did him!" [16]So they sent to Joseph and said: "Before your father died, he gave us these instructions: [17]'Thus you shall say to Joseph: Please forgive the criminal wrongdoing of your brothers, who treated you harmfully.' So now please forgive the crime that we, the servants of the God of your father, committed." When they said this to him, Joseph broke into tears. [18]Then his brothers also proceeded to fling themselves down before him and said, "We are your slaves!" [19]But Joseph replied to them: "Do not fear. Can I take the place of God? [20]Even though you meant harm to me, God meant it for good, to achieve this present end, the survival of many people. [21]So now, do not fear. I will provide for you and for your children." By thus speaking kindly to them, he reassured them.

[22]Joseph remained in Egypt, together with his father's household. He lived a hundred and ten years. [23]He saw Ephraim's children to the third generation, and the children of Manasseh's son Machir were also born on Joseph's knees.

Death of Joseph

[24]Joseph said to his brothers: "I am about to die. God will surely take care of you and lead you up from this land to the land that he promised on oath to Abraham, Isaac and Jacob." [25]Then, putting the sons of Israel under oath, he continued, "When God thus takes care of you, you must bring my bones up from this place." [26]Joseph died at the age of a hundred and ten. He was embalmed and laid to rest in a coffin in Egypt.

CONCLUSION

Our journey through Genesis began with God's creation of the universe and the first humans, whose early efforts to live in relationship with God and each other formed the basis of life within the human community. The story narrowed its focus from the universal to the family of one couple, Abraham and Sarah. Each time the people took missteps, God took action to reestablish the balance between the divine and human, and within the human community.

Throughout all these events God continued to provide for the peoples' needs. The ancestors were far from perfect or worthy. God guided them, with all their dignity and their frailty, in their comings and goings. Joseph summarized it for his brothers when he pointed out that God uses our actions to achieve the divine end (50:19-20). God continues to use our actions, redeeming what is evil and celebrating what is good. Genesis offers us the models; our lives continue the saga.

EXPLORING LESSON FIVE

1. What finally moves Joseph to reveal himself to his brothers (45:1-3)? (See 44:14-34.)

   He missed his father

2. What larger purpose does Joseph see at work behind the evil his brothers have done (45:4-8)?

   God sent him to Egypt

3. How have any unfortunate or painful events in your life helped you see and value what is truly important in life? (See Rom 8:28; 2 Cor 1:5-7; James 1:2-4.)

4. Why would it be important at this time in Jacob's life for God to give him a vision at Beer-sheba (46:1-4)? (See 35:12.)

   Here I am → same as Abraham + Isaac

5. Jacob describes himself and his ancestors as "wayfarers" (47:9). Why are Christians able to describe themselves in the same manner? (See 2 Cor 5:6; 1 Pet 1:1, 17; 2:11; Heb 13:14.)

   Life is a journey w/ many travels

Lesson Five

6. How do you think the people of Joseph's time would have regarded his land policy (47:13-26)? How would it be regarded today?

He saved them

7. Why do Jacob's first three sons, Reuben, Simeon, and Levi, receive more of a curse than a blessing from Jacob (49:1-7)? (See 34:25; 35:22.)

They were passed over for Judah

8. How is Jacob's blessing of Judah indicative of the future importance of King David and his heirs (49:9-10)? (See 2 Sam 7:1-17.)

lineage

9. What do you find most memorable or significant in the colorful Genesis saga of Abraham's offspring (chs. 21–50)?

Esau + Jacob

10. If you were writing a saga about your own ancestral family, at what key points would you emphasize God's presence and work among you?

CLOSING PRAYER

Prayer

"Even though you meant harm to me, God meant it for good . . ."   (Gen 50:20)

God of all that is and ever will be, we praise you. As you continue to fashion your people, we stand ready to be counted among them. You have the power to transform pain and wrongdoing so that redemption might be found. We pray for the capacity to cooperate with your grace, and we pray for the needs of those we love, especially . . .

PRAYING WITH YOUR GROUP

Because we know that the Bible allows us to hear God's voice, prayer provides the context for our study and sharing. By speaking and listening to God and each other, the discussion often grows to more deeply bond us to one another and to God.

At *the beginning and end of each lesson* simple prayers are provided for individual use, and also may be used within the group setting. Most of the closing prayers provided with each lesson relate directly to a theme from that lesson and encourage you to pray together for people and events in your local community.

Of course, there are many ways to center ourselves in God's presence as we gather together in groups around the word of God. We provide some additional suggestions here knowing you and your group will make prayer a priority as part of your gathering. These are simply alternative ways to pray if your group would like to try something different from those prayers provided in the previous pages.

Conversational Prayer

This form of prayer allows for the group members to pray in their own words in a way that is not intimidating. The group leader begins with Step One, inviting all to focus on the presence of Christ among them. After a few moments of quiet, the group leader invites anyone in the group to voice a prayer or two of thanksgiving; once that is complete, then anyone who has personal intentions may pray in their own words for their needs; finally, the group prays for the needs of others.

A suggested process:
In your own words, speak simple and short prayers to allow time for others to add their voices.

Focus on one "step" at a time, not worrying about praying for everything in your mental list at once.

Step One	Visualize Christ. Welcome him. Imagine him present with you in your group. Allow time for some silence.
Step Two	Gratitude opens our hearts. Use simple words such as, "Thank you, Lord, for . . ."
Step Three	Pray for your own needs knowing that others will pray with you. Be specific and honest. Use "I" and "me" language.

Step Four	Pray for others by name, with love.
	You may voice your agreement ("Yes, Lord").
	End with gratitude for sharing concerns.

Praying Like Ignatius

St. Ignatius Loyola, whose life and ministry is the foundation of the Jesuit community, invites us to enter into Scripture texts in order to experience the scenes, especially scenes of the gospels or other narrative parts of Scripture. Simply put, this is a method of creatively imagining the scene, viewing it from the inside, and asking God to meet you there. Most often, this is a personal form of prayer but in a group setting, some of its elements can be helpful if you allow time for this process.

A suggested process:

- Select a scene from the chapters in the particular lesson.

- Read that scene out loud in the group, followed by some quiet time.

- Ask group members to place themselves in the scene (as a character, or as an onlooker) so that they can imagine the emotions, responses, and thinking that may have taken place. Notice the details and the tone, and imagine the interaction with the Lord that is taking place.

- Share with the group any insights that came to you in this quiet imagining.

- Allow each person in the group to thank God for some insight and to pray about some request that may have surfaced.

Sacred Reading (or Lectio Divina)

This method of prayer invites us to "listen with the ear of the heart" as St. Benedict's rule would say. We listen to the words and the phrasing, asking God to speak to our innermost being. Again, this method of prayer is most often used in an individual setting but may also be used in an adapted way within a group.

A suggested process:

- Select a scene from the chapters in the particular lesson.

- Read the scene out loud in the group, perhaps two times.

- Ask group members to ponder a word or phrase that stands out to them.

- The group members could then simply speak the word or phrase as a kind of litany of what was meaningful for your group.

- Allow time for more silence to ponder the words that were heard, asking God to reveal to you what message you are meant to hear, how God is speaking to you.

- Follow up with spoken intentions at the close of this group time.

REFLECTING ON SCRIPTURE

Reading Scripture is an opportunity not simply to learn new information but to listen to God who loves you. Pray that the same Holy Spirit who guided the formation of Scripture will inspire you to correctly understand what you read, and empower you to make what you read a part of your life.

The inspired word of God contains layers of meaning. As you make your way through passages of Scripture, whether studying a book of the Bible or focusing on a biblical theme, you may find it helpful to ask yourself these four questions:

What does the Scripture passage say?
Read the passage slowly and reflectively. Become familiar with it. If the passage you are reading is a narrative, carefully observe the characters and the plot. Use your imagination to picture the scene or enter into it.

What does the Scripture passage mean?
Read the footnotes in your Bible and the commentary provided to help you understand what the sacred writers intended and what God wants to communicate by means of their words.

What does the Scripture passage mean to me?
Meditate on the passage. God's word is living and powerful. What is God saying to you? How does the Scripture passage apply to your life today?

What am I going to do about it?
Try to discover how God may be challenging you in this passage. An encounter with God contains a challenge to know God's will and follow it more closely in daily life. Ask the Holy Spirit to inspire not only your mind but your life with this living word.